Cambridge Elements

Elements in Gender and Politics
edited by
Tiffany D. Barnes
University of Texas at Austin
Diana Z. O'Brien
Washington University in St. Louis

WHAT'S HAPPENED TO THE GENDER GAP IN POLITICAL ACTIVITY?

Social Structure, Politics, and Participation in the United States

Shauna L. Shames
Rutgers University – Camden

Sara Morell
The College of New Jersey

Ashley Jardina
University of Virginia

Kay Lehman Schlozman
Boston College

Nancy Burns
University of Michigan

Shaftesbury Road, Cambridge CB2 8EA, United Kingdom

One Liberty Plaza, 20th Floor, New York, NY 10006, USA

477 Williamstown Road, Port Melbourne, VIC 3207, Australia

314–321, 3rd Floor, Plot 3, Splendor Forum, Jasola District Centre, New Delhi – 110025, India

103 Penang Road, #05–06/07, Visioncrest Commercial, Singapore 238467

Cambridge University Press is part of Cambridge University Press & Assessment, a department of the University of Cambridge.

We share the University's mission to contribute to society through the pursuit of education, learning and research at the highest international levels of excellence.

www.cambridge.org
Information on this title: www.cambridge.org/9781009509664

DOI: 10.1017/9781009330626

© Shauna L. Shames, Sara Morell, Ashley Jardina, Kay Lehman Schlozman and Nancy Burns 2025

This publication is in copyright. Subject to statutory exception and to the provisions of relevant collective licensing agreements, with the exception of the Creative Commons version the link for which is provided below, no reproduction of any part may take place without the written permission of Cambridge University Press & Assessment.

An online version of this work is published at doi.org/10.1017/9781009330626 under a Creative Commons Open Access license CC-BY-NC-ND 4.0 which permits re-use, distribution and reproduction in any medium for non-commercial purposes providing appropriate credit to the original work is given. You may not distribute derivative works without permission. To view a copy of this license, visit https://creativecommons.org/licenses/by-nc-nd/4.0

When citing this work, please include a reference to the DOI 10.1017/9781009330626

First published 2025

A catalogue record for this publication is available from the British Library

ISBN 978-1-009-50966-4 Hardback
ISBN 978-1-009-33063-3 Paperback
ISSN 2753-8117 (online)
ISSN 2753-8109 (print)

Additional resources for this publication at www.cambridge.org/Shames

Cambridge University Press & Assessment has no responsibility for the persistence or accuracy of URLs for external or third-party internet websites referred to in this publication and does not guarantee that any content on such websites is, or will remain, accurate or appropriate.

What's Happened to the Gender Gap in Political Activity?

Social Structure, Politics, and Participation in the United States

Elements in Gender and Politics

DOI: 10.1017/9781009330626
First published online: February 2025

Shauna L. Shames
Rutgers University – Camden

Sara Morell
The College of New Jersey

Ashley Jardina
University of Virginia

Kay Lehman Schlozman
Boston College

Nancy Burns
University of Michigan

Author for correspondence: Shauna L. Shames, shauna.shames@rutgers.edu

> **Abstract:** This Element considers changes to the long-standing pattern in U.S. politics that women are less politically active than men. On one hand, the gender gap in political activity beyond voting has disappeared. On the other, the disparity remains when it comes to political money. What is the explanation? The Element begins with politics – both the long-term increase in women occupying political positions and the way that trends/events like MeToo, the defeat of Hillary Clinton, and Donald Trump's performative masculinity made gender salient. It then turns to social structural changes, examining in particular women's relative gains in income and, especially, education. Paying consistent attention to intersectional differences among men and among women, based on political party, race, or ethnicity, the authors find the explanation of these trends to be rooted not in politics, but rather in social structure. This title is also available as Open Access on Cambridge Core.

Keywords: women, gender, politics, participation, gender gap

© Shauna L. Shames, Sara Morell, Ashley Jardina, Kay Lehman Schlozman and Nancy Burns 2025

ISBNs: 9781009509664 (HB), 9781009330633 (PB), 9781009330626 (OC)
ISSNs: 2753-8117 (online), 2753-8109 (print)

Contents

1 The Changing Gender Gap in Political Participation   1

2 The Puzzle and the Model   14

3 What about Politics?   23

4 Is It Social-Structural Resources?   43

5 The Dollar Gap   59

6 Epilogue   70

    References   74

1 The Changing Gender Gap in Political Participation

The decades since the emergence of the second wave women's movement in the late 1960s have witnessed significant developments in American politics and society. Expansion of coeducational colleges and universities. Advances toward equal pay. Title IX of the Education Amendments. Conflicts over reproductive rights. More women in state legislatures and the U.S. Congress. The first woman on the Supreme Court. The first woman to be nominated for president by a major political party. Amid these momentous changes, one important change has gone unnoticed: the closing of the narrow, but long-standing, gender disparity in political participation with women slightly less active than men.

Until the ratification of the Nineteenth Amendment in 1920, nearly a century and a half after the nation's founding, women were not guaranteed the right to vote on a national basis. After their enfranchisement, women's political participation continued to lag behind men's. They went to the polls less frequently and engaged at lower rates in other forms of political activity like contacting elected officials, donating to candidates and parties, and participating in campaigns. In short, for most of U.S. history, a gender gap in participation was a feature of American politics. Nearly five decades ago, a comprehensive study of citizen political activity observed, "The finding that men are more likely to participate in politics is one of the most thoroughly substantiated in social science" (Milbrath and Goel 1977, p. 116).

But sometime in the latter decades of the twentieth century, the persistent gap in most forms of participation narrowed or closed. And for some forms, like voting, a gap reemerged, but with women participating at rates *greater* than men. In the sections to come, we revisit women's levels of political activity relative to men's. We ask – and, in the search for answers, examine a small mountain of data – this central question: Over the past five decades, how have women's relative rates of political activity changed, and what explains these changes?[1]

We focus on three forms of participation – voting, campaign activity (including working for a candidate or attending a political rally), and making contributions to candidates and campaigns.[2] These participatory acts differ in important ways. For one, Americans are much more likely to go to the polls than to get involved in campaigns or to make political donations. For another, the costs of engaging in these forms of political activity differ. Compared to voting,

---

[1] For a less comprehensive effort to answer this project's central question, see Burns et al. (2018). For a literature review on gender gaps in electoral participation in the United States, see Burns, Jardina, and Yadon (2017). For an overview of gender gaps in participatory acts among young people across European countries, see Grasso and Smith (2022).

[2] For discussion of why we focus on these three activities only, see Section 2.1.

campaign participation generally entails a greater time commitment, and donating to a political candidate or party requires financial resources.[3]

Looking over the past half-century, we find an overall convergence by gender in rates of political participation, but the patterns differ for these three ways of taking part. Sometime in the 1980s, the traditional gender gap in electoral turnout reversed – women became somewhat more likely than men to go to the polls (Wolbrecht and Corder 2020; CAWP 2023b). Roughly a quarter of a century later, with the critical exception of campaign donations, women's political participation deficit disappeared, a development that has gone largely unnoticed by political scientists.

What accounts for the narrowing – and, in the case of voting, the reversal – of the participation gender gap? We embed our inquiry in the larger picture of American politics and society and ask: Is the reduction in the gender gap the result of growing interest in politics and political mobilization, sparked by the greater number of visible women in politics and the growing number of women contesting and winning elections? Or is it the result of structural changes related to socioeconomic status (SES), in particular, women's increased level of educational attainment and the lessening of the income gender gap? To anticipate our central conclusion, contrary to our expectations, we do not find even a partial explanation in politics. Instead, convergence between women and men in political participation seems rooted in women's relative educational and income gains.

1.1 Participation, Democracy, and Equality

It is essential to political life in a democracy that citizens have the right to participate freely. Through their participation, citizens can influence who holds governmental power and what they do with it, communicate preferences and needs for government action to public officials, and hold officials accountable. Scholars of political participation do not always define it in exactly the same way. We adopt a quite conventional definition: "activity that has the intent or effect of influencing government action – either directly by affecting the making

---

[3] An extensive literature in political science explores the various kinds of political activities in which individuals take part and the distinctive configurations of factors that help to explain them. For a recent overview, see Schlozman and Brady (2022). Among the many notable works are Verba and Nie (1972); Milbrath and Goel (1977); Wolfinger and Rosenstone (1980); Junn (1991); Rosenstone and Hansen (1993); Leighley (1995); Verba, Schlozman, and Brady (1995); Nie, Junn, and Stehlik-Barry (1996); Brady (1999); Skocpol and Fiorina (1999); Burns, Schlozman, and Verba (2001); Schlozman (2002); Zukin et al. (2006); Dalton and Klingemann (2007, Part VI); Ramakrishnan and Bloemraad (2008); Leighley (2010, Part III); Gerber et al. (2011); Leighley and Nagler (2014); Campbell (2016); Dinesen et al. (2016); Krupnikov and Levine (2016); Dalton (2017); Holbein (2017); Schur, Ameri, and Adya (2017); Blais and Achen (2019); and Green and Gerber (2019).

or implementation of public policy or indirectly by influencing the selection of people who make those policies" (Verba, Schlozman, and Brady 1995, p. 38).

This capacious definition encompasses the many ways that citizens in affluent democracies can take part politically. It includes political acts that may require time or money; acts that may be performed online or off; acts that individuals may undertake alone or with others; as well as acts that seek direct influence through expressions of preferences aimed at policy-makers and those that seek indirect influence through participation in the electoral process. Participatory acts include, most importantly, voting, as well as contacting a public official, signing a petition, attending a protest, joining a political party or an organization that takes stands in politics, working in an electoral campaign, attending a rally, and donating money to a campaign or political cause. In its emphasis on doing, our definition excludes activities that entail following or talking about politics, such as reading about politics in newspapers and discussing politics with friends or through social media. In focusing on action aimed at public authorities, it omits engaging in civic life in ways that bypass the usual institutions of politics and government, for example, by taking part in product boycotts (e.g., Jacobs, Cook, and Delli Carpini 2009; Micheletti and McFarland 2010).

Why do we care about inequalities in political participation? Students of democratic political participation point to multiple benefits that accrue to those who take part. Political involvement by citizens cultivates capacities for activity both within and outside of politics; activists are better able to define their wants and needs and to pursue them effectively. Perhaps more fundamentally, equal political participation is the underpinning of equal protection of interests in a democracy. When unequal participation among individuals produces unequal voice among politically relevant groups, and when unequal political voice persists over time, the potential violation of democratic equality becomes that much more serious.

This principle from democratic theory is especially relevant because men and women as groups differ somewhat in their political attitudes, partisan leanings, and vote choices. Reflecting multiple factors, including the continuing weight of unequal social and economic gender roles, women and men as groups tend to have different preferences about and needs for government policy and action (see, for example, Sapiro 1986; Burns and Gallagher 2010; Lizotte 2020; and Pew 2022). Women are, on average, more liberal than men on issues like the use of force in international affairs, regulating guns, sexual harassment, and social welfare benefit generosity. Women are also more likely to identify with the

Democratic Party and to vote for Democratic candidates,[4] a difference that engages race or ethnicity and, more recently, education as well as gender (Junn and Matsuoka 2020).

In an era of ideologically divergent and electorally matched parties, even narrow disparities may be consequential when linked to group-based deficits in participation. Gender differences in partisan choices and political attitudes are not particularly large and are dwarfed, for example, by the chasm that divides the issue preferences and electoral choices of Black and white voters (Kinder and Sanders 1996; White and Laird 2020; Jardina and Ollerenshaw 2022). Still, gender disparities in political activity can have a meaningful aggregate impact on political outcomes, whether through the results of elections or the resultant policies that have consequences for women's and men's lives. More generally, if women and men – or the members of any other groups with different political preferences and needs for government action or inaction – are differentially active in politics, there are potential implications for the principles of democratic equality and equal protection of interests.

1.2 Studying the Participation Gap Intersectionally

One challenge scholars confront is the tension between understanding gender as a locus of inequality and the impossibility of isolating gender from individuals' other politically relevant attributes (Combahee 1977; hooks 1981; Crenshaw 1990; Brown 2014; Cassese, Barnes, and Branton 2015; Brown and Gershon 2016; Hancock 2016). Our inquiry into disparities in political participation seeks to explain what has happened in the United States in terms of women and men as groups. We recognize, however, that women and men are diverse across every factor that might have consequences for both participation and political preferences – for example, social class, age, partisanship, religious commitments and practices, family situation, and, especially, race and ethnicity. Some scholars consider it ill-advised to study women and men without further subdividing along other fault lines, especially race or ethnicity (see, e.g., Simien 2006 and 2007; Junn and Brown 2008; Kim and Junn 2024). We therefore take an intersectional approach by examining changes in participation not only for all men and women, but also separately for subgroups defined by race and

---

[4] The persistent gender gap in vote choice, with more men more likely to prefer Republican candidates, emerged in 1980 and generally ranges 7–10 percentage points (Box-Steffensmeier, De Boef, and Lin 2004; Whitaker 2008; CAWP 2023a; Wolbrecht and Corder 2020). This gap also obtains, to varying degrees, across racial and ethnic groups (Lien 1998). Among Black Americans the gender gap is attenuated by a historically strong allegiance to the Democratic Party (White and Laird 2020). For Hispanic Americans, differences in immigration experiences may explain greater support for the Democratic Party among Latinas versus Latinos (Bejarano 2013).

ethnicity. Regrettably, our data strategy permits robust analysis of just six groups:[5] women and men in the three largest groups defined by race or ethnicity in the United States: white, Black, and Hispanic[6] Americans.

The sociopolitical experiences of Black and Hispanic Americans have differed from those of white Americans in multiple ways with implications for participatory inequalities. For much of American history, public authorities ranging from legislators to sheriffs to judges used law, custom, and violence to erect barriers to the political participation of Black Americans, such that their political incorporation was seriously delayed (Philpot and Walton 2014). Perhaps the most notorious barriers were the multiple mechanisms used to disenfranchise Black men and women in the South, who were not effectively granted suffrage until the Voting Rights Act of 1965. Similarly, many Hispanic Americans were not granted protections from efforts to limit their ability to vote until the extension of the Voting Rights Act in 1975, which provided protections for "language minorities."

Moreover, pervasive and persistent racial discrimination kept Black and Hispanic Americans from equal access with white Americans to such critical participatory resources as education and income. Because income and, especially, education are related to the capacity to be active in politics as well as to gender, racial and ethnic (and other intersectional) differences in political activity derive, at least in part, from group differences in SES.[7] That SES disadvantage figures in the explanation of group differences in participation does not, however, diminish the importance of other identities and attributes for the understanding of group-based participatory disparities. On the contrary, the

---

[5] Our primary data source, the American National Election Study (ANES), contains insufficient cases for analysis of individuals identifying as multiracial, Native/Indigenous, or Asian American/API, which produces a serious gap in American politics research. Many scholars have been working to address this lacuna (Barreto et al. 2018), including through the development of a large-scale representative survey of Asian Americans—the National Asian American Survey (Ramakrishnan et al. 2008; Ramakrishnan et al. 2016). See Wong et al. (2011) for a comprehensive analysis of Asian American participation using these data, and also Lien (1994); Lien (2001); Lien et al. (2001); Wong, Lien, and Conway (2005); Jacob (2006); Junn and Masuoka (2008); Phillips and Lee (2018); Masuoka, Ramanathan, and Junn (2019); Sanchez, Masuoka, and Abrams (2019); and Chan and Phoenix (2020). Other scholars are making inroads into the study of Native American populations using public opinion data, e.g., Peterson (1997); Huyser, Sanchez, and Vargas (2017); Herrick and Mendez (2019); and Sanchez and Foxworth (2022).

[6] We recognize that there is no agreement on the appropriate term to refer to those of Hispanic or Latin American descent. Because the principal sources of data on which we rely, the American National Election Studies and the U.S. Census, ask about "Hispanic" ethnicity, we use that term. We should note that, although Hispanic Americans can be of any race, when we discuss "white respondents," we are referring to non-Hispanic white respondents only.

[7] Burns, Schlozman, and Verba (2001, chap. 11) find that disparities in such participatory resources as education, income, and civic skills go far in explaining differences in political activity among intersectional groups defined by gender and race or ethnicity (for contrary findings, see Holman 2016).

SES advantages enjoyed by men and whites are a legacy of historical experiences and discriminatory processes that are rooted in group membership and that date back centuries. Besides, whatever their origins, differences in political activity across both race or ethnicity and gender mean that public officials hear much more from some people than from others.

In sum, that race or ethnicity and gender operate simultaneously to structure political experiences renders unwise investigations that consider these identities in isolation (Brown 2014). Our examination of participation therefore takes into consideration the likelihood that the timing and size of any gender gaps across various forms of participation may not be the same for all racial and ethnic groups. These intersectional groups defined by gender and race or ethnicity are also, themselves, fundamentally shaped by diverse material and social realities, including – but not limited to – marital status, educational attainment, income and wealth deprivation, immigration status, or incarceration status, that can shape individuals' propensities to take part politically.

1.3 Changing Gender and Intersectional Disparities in Political Participation

We launch our inquiry by considering how the gender gap in political activity over the last two generations has changed over time with respect to voting, campaign participation, and making campaign contributions. Our investigation relies on data from the American National Election Studies (ANES), a set of nationally representative public opinion surveys with impressive longevity. The ANES studies constitute the most reliable source of data about Americans' political behavior and attitudes, although using these data does involve several methodological caveats and limitations, which we discuss in detail in Section 2.1 and Appendix A.[8] The studies, in which nationally representative samples of Americans have been interviewed before and after every presidential election since 1952, provide invaluable insight into who participates in politics and why. And, because the ANES surveys contain items with identical wording over several decades, they are an irreplaceable resource for our inquiry.

We begin with the most common and visible form of political engagement: voting in presidential elections. Figure 1 shows the trajectory of changes in the gender gap in voter turnout from 1964 to 2020 for men and women and, then, separately for men and women by race and ethnicity. We note below the figure

---

[8] Replication files for this project will be available through The University of Michigan's Deep Blue Data Repository, under the authors' names, at https://deepblue.lib.umich.edu/data/about. Online appendices are at www.cambridge.org/Shames

the years in which the gender difference in turnout is statistically significant. The top-left panel of Figure 1, which presents data for all women and men, shows a gender gap to men's advantage in the presidential elections between 1964 and 1976. In those years, men turned out at rates between 4 and 9 percentage points higher than women. The gap closes by 1980 and, with the exception of 1988 and 2000, does not reappear in subsequent elections.[9] In both 2008 and 2016, women voted at rates greater than men.

We also consider the gender gap in voting among white, Black, and Hispanic Americans. Our efforts here require some data caveats, which we discuss in detail in Section 2. Prior to 2008, the ANES included only small samples of Black and Hispanic respondents. In fact, we do not begin our examination of Hispanic participation until 1988 when the number of Hispanic respondents surpassed 100. As a result, we proceed with caution in interpreting trends among these groups in earlier years.

The top-right panel of Figure 1 reveals that turnout patterns for white voters look similar to the results just reviewed for all men and women. Compared to white men, white women were less likely to vote in 1964, 1972, and 1976. Between 1980 and 2004, white men and women were equally likely to go the polls, and in 2008 and 2020, white women surpassed white men in turnout. Of note, in the ANES data, the narrowing and ultimate reversal of the gender gap happens later than in U.S. Census data, which indicate a slight, but persistent, turnout advantage for white women beginning in 1984 (Wolbrecht and Corder 2020; CAWP 2023b).

The bottom-left panel of Figure 1 presents turnout trends for Black women and men. A significant gender gap appears only in 1968 and 1976, with Black women turning out at rates lower than Black men. From 1980 onward, ANES data show Black men and women turning out at equal rates. Consistent with earlier work that finds that Black women have been just as, if not more, politically engaged than Black men in the post–Civil Rights era, U.S. Census data show Black women having a persistent turnout advantage starting in 1980 (Baxter and Lansing 1983; Harris, Sinclair-Chapman, and McKenzie 2005; Robnett and Bany 2011; CAWP 2023b). The disparity in turnout between Black men and women in the Census data is greater than that between white or Hispanic men and women, a finding consistent with other research (Cole and Stewart 1996).

The bottom-right panel of Figure 1 shows trends in voting rates among Hispanic Americans. Significant gender differences in voting appear only in

---

[9] For further discussion of the ANES estimates of voter turnout over time, and discussion of how these compare to other sources of data, please see Section A of the online Appendix.

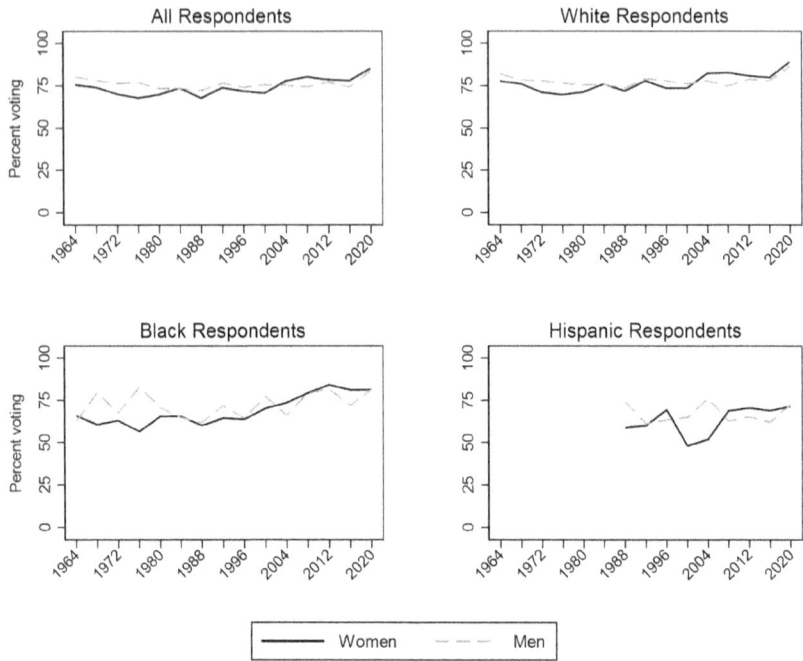

Figure 1 Percent voting in presidential elections by gender and race or ethnicity: 1964–2020

Data from the ANES cumulative file and the 2020 ANES (weighted). Analysis among Hispanic respondents begins with 1988 when the number of Hispanic respondents in the sample broached 100.

Differences between women and men are statistically significant in the following years at the $p<=0.05$ threshold (bolded years at the $p<=0.10$ threshold) among:
Full sample: 1964, **1968**, 1972, 1976, 1988, **2000**, 2008, 2016
White respondents: **1964**, 1972, 1976, 2008, 2020
Black respondents: 1968, 1976
Hispanic respondents: **1988**, 2004

1988 and 2004, when Hispanic men turned out at greater rates than Hispanic women. From 2008 and continuing to 201[[6]], Hispanic women's voting rates appeared to surpass those of Hispanic men's (a finding consistent with data from the Latino National Survey; Bejarano 2013), although the difference between the two groups across these years is not statistically significant in the ANES.

In sum, we see some evidence of a gender gap in voting across racial and ethnic groups, with women voting at lower rates than men before 1980. ANES data show the gender gap closing across racial and ethnic groups sometime in the 1980s (earlier for Black and White Americans than for Hispanic

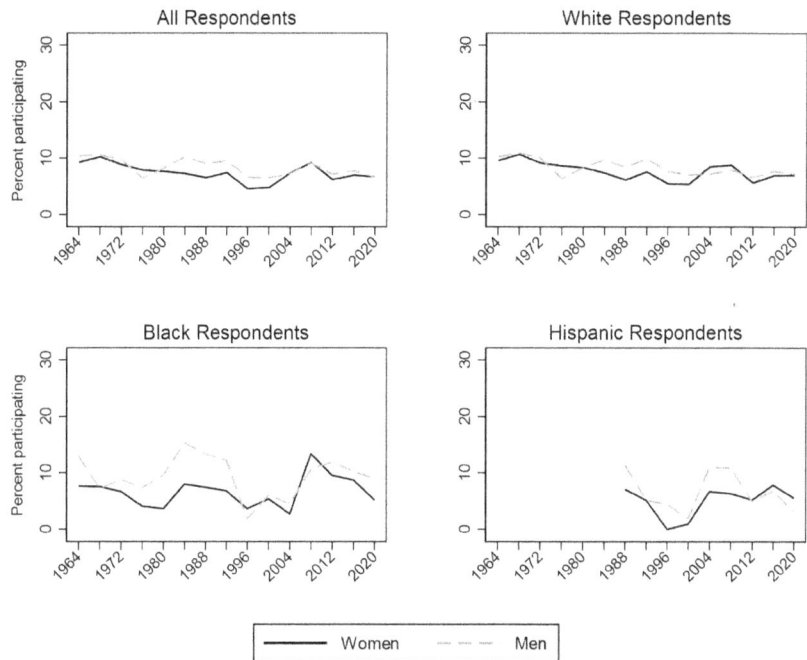

Figure 2 Percent participating in campaign activities* by gender and race or ethnicity: 1964–2020

Data from the ANES cumulative file and the 2020 ANES (weighted). Analysis among Hispanic respondents begins in 1988 when the number of Hispanic respondents in the sample broached 100.

* Includes attending a political meeting/rally or working for a candidate.
Differences between women and men are statistically significant in the following years at the $p<=0.05$ threshold (bolded years at the $p<=0.10$ threshold) among:
Full sample: 1984, 1988, **1992**, **1996**
White respondents: **1976, 1984, 1988, 1992**
Hispanic respondents: **1996, 2008**
Black respondents: (none)

Americans). Census data show these turnout advantages happening even earlier for women in each of these racial and ethnic groups (see Appendix A for discussion of trends in participation across other data sources).

Figure 2 presents longitudinal data about participation in political campaigns. One immediate difference between campaign participation and voting is that, across groups, rates of campaign participation are much lower. In most years, fewer than 15 percent of Americans report engaging in this type of political activity. The top-left panel shows the trends in campaign participation for all women and men. Between 1984 and 1996, there is a small, but significant, gender gap, with men more active. After 1996, however, there is no identifiable gender difference in campaign participation for men and women as groups.

We observe some differences in these trends when we disaggregate by race and ethnicity, also shown in Figure 2. Among white respondents, the gender gap favoring men is evident beginning in 1984 and loses statistical significance in 1992. For Black Americans, while there appears to be some gender gap in campaign participation between 1972 and 1992, in no year is the difference between men and women statistically significant. There is more variability in the gap among Hispanic respondents over time, but the difference between men and women in this group is significant only in 1996 and 2008 – consistent with earlier work, which finds few consistent gender differences in Hispanics' campaign participation (Schlozman, Burns, and Verba 1994). Unlike voting, campaign participation does not show any female advantage, although the previous gap, which advantaged men, had largely closed within all groups defined by gender and race or ethnicity.

Figure 3 presents analogous data about donating money to a political party or candidate.[10] Again, we see that rates of engaging in this form of participation are low. In most years, under 20 percent of Americans report such activity. The top-left panel of Figure 3 shows a persistent gender gap between 1964 and 2000, with men more likely to donate. The gap briefly disappeared for a while before reappearing in 2012, but in 2016 and 2020, men and women reported donating at similar rates.

Disaggregating by race and ethnicity shows that, among white Americans, men are more likely than women to donate for much of the time series. Among Black Americans, we do not find a statistically significant gender gap in making donations after 1992. Among Hispanic Americans, although men's rates of making contributions surpass women's in most years, the difference is statistically significant only in 2016. While perhaps surprising, the absence of a consistent, significant gender gap in donating among Hispanics is consistent with prior research that uses the Latino National Political Survey (Montoya 1997 and 2000; Montoya, Hardy-Fanta, and Garcia 2000).

One key limitation of the ANES data for understanding political donations is that the survey does not ask respondents who reported donating *how much* they gave. When it comes to making contributions, if the bank account permits, it is possible to multiply the volume of participatory input substantially. Still, most people make

---

[10] The ANES cumulative data file combines two questions from each individual survey, which separately ask whether the respondent contributed to support campaigns – by giving money either to a political party or to an individual candidate. Question wording has remained the same since 1988.

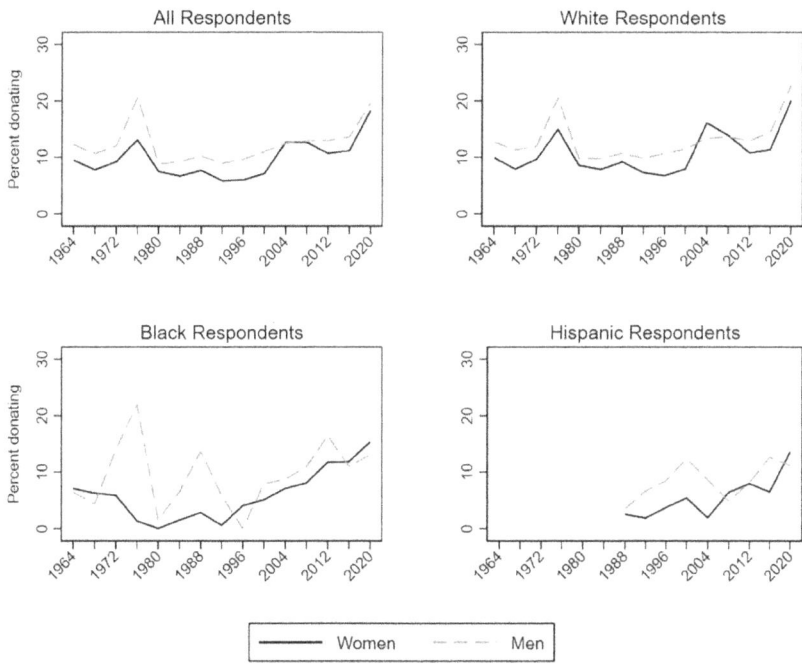

Figure 3 Percent donating to a political party or candidate by gender and race or ethnicity: 1964–2020

Data from the ANES cumulative file and the 2020 ANES (weighted). Analysis among Hispanic respondents begins with 1988 when the number of Hispanic respondents in the ANES sample broached 100.

Differences between women and men are statistically significant in the following years at the p<=0.05 threshold (bolded years at the p<=0.10 threshold) among:
Full sample: **1964**, **1968**, *1972, 1976, 1984,* **1988**, *1992, 1996, 2000, 2012*
White respondents: 1968, 1976, **1992**, *1996, 2000, 2016,* **2020**
Black respondents: **1972**, *1976,* **1984**, *1988, 1992*
Hispanic respondents: **2016**

no contributions, and among those who donate, the vast majority make only modest political donations, well under the federal limit. However, a series of federal judicial decisions in recent decades has made it easier for individuals and organizations to donate very large sums, meaning that a tiny number of Americans who command the resources to do so now make truly enormous campaign contributions. The ability of a handful of contributors to donate millions means that only a very small number of people are responsible for a substantial proportion of total campaign dollars (OpenSecrets 2023a; see also Skocpol 2017; Page, Seawright, and Lacombe 2018; and Persily, Bauer, and Ginsberg 2018). We delve further into the special case of big-dollar donating in Section 5.

1.4 Explaining Changing Gender Disparities in Political Activity

Although the patterns are different for the three kinds of political activity we are considering, in each case where there was once a gap, over time men's participatory advantage eroded. How do we explain the changes in the long-standing disparities between women and men in these forms of political activity? And why would a small, but long-standing, gender gap in campaign participation close rather abruptly in the early 2000s? These questions animate the remainder of our inquiry.

We have already referred to the fact that political activity is multivariate, the result of many factors working together. For the gender gap in activity to diminish, at least one of two things must happen: either women's access to one or more factors that facilitate political activity must increase relative to men's, or the relative impact of one or more participatory factors must change in such a way as to diminish men's advantage or enhance women's. Our careful multivariate analysis of what has happened over time involves a number of strategies and sources of data, described in detail in Section 2.

To account for the patterns just described, we consider the potential role of significant political and social trends in Sections 3 and 4. We begin with an obvious point of departure in Section 3: politics itself. Over the last half-century, gender has entered American politics in multiple ways: for example, the decision in *Roe* v. *Wade* and its later reversal; the ultimately unsuccessful campaign for the Equal Rights Amendment; the Hill-Thomas Senate hearings that brought attention to the issue of sexual harassment and led to the Year of the Woman and the expansion of women's presence in federal electoral politics; the elevation of Justice Sandra Day O'Connor, House Speaker Nancy Pelosi, and Vice President Kamala Harris to high-visibility positions that women had never before occupied; the nomination of Hillary Clinton, the first woman to run for president on a national party ticket, and her Electoral College defeat by Donald Trump, the target of multiple accusations of sexual assault whose campaigns and presidency were characterized by unprecedented levels of performative masculinity and misogynistic rhetoric. Have these developments spurred women to take political action?

In Section 3, we also focus on the implications for political participation of the growth over time in the number of citizens whose immediate political environment includes a woman contesting or holding visible public office such as governor, senator, or member of the House of Representatives. Earlier research (Burns, Schlozman, and Verba 2001, chap. 13) showed that a significant component of the explanation of the gender gap in political activity in the 1990s was women's deficit with respect to a set of psychological orientations to politics in which political interest figures importantly. In Section 3, we return to the complicated role of electoral interest in the chain of variables associated with participation.

In Section 4, we consider long-term social structural changes. Studies of citizen participation in the United States have long shown that a cluster of factors related to social class – in particular, education and income – influence political participation, a pattern that appears, though is usually less pronounced, in other affluent democracies (Verba, Nie, and Kim 1978; Verba, Schlozman, and Brady 1995). One consequential long-term social trend is the fact that, for more than a generation, women in the United States have been more likely than men to graduate from college. More complicated, but still potentially consequential for shrinking the gender gap in participation, are varying patterns of gender differences in family income, which are in turn related to complex changes in family structure, workforce participation, and earnings. Focusing on the erosion of men's advantage over women with respect to education and income, Section 4 investigates structural resources as a potential answer to the question of explaining the changing contours of the participatory gender gap.

In Section 5, we discuss a second continuing political trend with possibly contrary implications for gender disparities in participation: the evolution of the American campaign finance regime. Compared to other affluent democracies, the American system of electoral finance avoids reliance on the public treasury and allows much greater latitude for unregulated individual giving. Beginning with *Buckley* v. *Valeo* (1976) and accelerated by *Citizens United* (2010), a series of federal court decisions has defined campaign giving as a form of free speech and corporations as people.[11] In the aftermath, an avalanche of huge sums, many of which cannot be traced, has poured into electoral politics. The result is that forms of the expression of political voice based on inputs of money have assumed greater relative weight in the bundle of participatory acts. Men have traditionally been (and remain) dominant among the high rollers in campaign giving. Even though women now do not lag substantially in the likelihood of having made a campaign donation of any size, the stupendous amounts given imply that the biggest contributors speak with a megaphone – and those super-contributors are disproportionately male.

We were surprised to find that the political changes we examine are not the key to the erosion of men's advantage with respect to three major forms of

---

[11] For discussion of recent judicial decisions that have created the current environment for campaign giving and the extent to which total giving at the federal level is dominated by a handful of very generous donors, see Schlozman, Brady, and Verba (2018), pp. 212–214; 244–250.

political activity. What does seem to make a difference is women's relative gains with respect to income and, especially, education.

1.5 Summary

In the sections to come, we consider possible explanations for the changes in long-standing patterns in which women have been less politically active than men. In particular, we ask whether the change is the product of shifts in resource acquisition or whether political factors account for these shifts. We begin with an explanation of our methods of investigation and sources of data (Section 2). We then turn to politics – both proximate political causes and long-term political trends – and the question of electoral interest and how it differs by gender (Section 3). We move to the larger picture of the American social structure and consider the ways in which shifts in long-term social and economic trends may have contributed to changes in rates of political activity for women and men as groups and for subgroups of women and men defined by race or ethnicity (Section 4). We conclude with a closer examination of the only form of political activity for which there is an ongoing gender gap, donating (Section 5). For this form of participation, the gender gap persists and, in some respects, has grown.

2 The Puzzle and the Model

In the time since we have had data to measure it, the gap in political participation between men and women in the United States has been small – just a few percentage points – but consistent, with men participating more than women. The size of the gap has changed over time; for some forms of participation, like voting, it began shrinking in the 1980s. For other participatory acts, such as taking part in political campaigns, the gap was small but steady before it closed rather abruptly in the early 2000s. Around this same time, the gender gap in making political donations closed for women and men, but it has since reopened in men's favor – and, considered from one perspective, may be widening.

When and why these changes occurred are the questions that motivate our central inquiry. To scholars of participation, it is indeed puzzling that so long-standing a group difference should diminish or even reverse without an obvious cause. In this work, we propose and test a variety of explanations for the notable changes in the gender gap in political participation. Our efforts involve a massive data analysis delving deeply into the significant changes in women's lives over the past six decades in the United States.

In this section, we describe the data we bring to bear to study the puzzle of gender differences in participation. We also explain our methodological approach to the analysis, including the model we use to estimate men's and women's political participation, and the tack we take for understanding the relationship between the factors predicting participation and their relationship to changing levels of engagement over time.

2.1 Using Data to Understand Men's and Women's Participation

With two exceptions, there is no systematic, public record keeping of political activity in the United States. The federal government and all states report information on campaign contributions (with wide variation in what counts as a "contribution" and what other information is reported). States also record whether someone who is registered to vote casts a ballot on election day. Otherwise, we have no official records of most forms of political activities, such as working in a campaign or contacting an elected official. In short, our knowledge of who participates politically largely comes from public opinion surveys.[12]

An important virtue of public opinion surveys is they usually include additional information about respondents' demographic characteristics, political identities, and political attitudes that researchers can use to understand who participates in politics and why. Throughout this text, to investigate the dynamics of the gender gap in political participation, we turn to what is considered the gold standard of public opinion studies: the American National Election Studies (Aldrich and McGraw 2011).

The ANES has been administered to national probability samples of American adults who have been interviewed, face-to-face, in every presidential election year since 1952.[13] The ANES survey instruments are benchmarks for best practices in survey methodology. The questions measuring political preferences and behavior are carefully designed, tested, and approved by boards composed of established public opinion researchers; interviewers are thoroughly trained; and careful attention is paid to the wording and order of questions included on the study. The ANES also prioritizes continuity by including the same well-designed measures of political attitudes and behaviors year after year. These advantages of the ANES allow us to engage in comprehensive and systematic study of the factors associated with voting, campaign participation, and donating for men and women over time.

---

[12] Privately owned "voter files" also provide detailed information about registered voters. They are limited in what information they can provide about participation because most do not have records of citizens who are not registered to vote. Furthermore, much of the demographic information they contain comes from predictive models, making them prone to errors and omissions (Igielnik et al. 2018).

[13] In later years, the ANES also added companion online samples. When available, we pool face-to-face and online samples.

Although the ANES is the only dataset that would allow us to undertake our longitudinal, multivariate analysis, it does have limitations. We must confine our focus to the three political activities that have been measured consistently in ANES surveys across time. These three encompass the most frequent political activity, going to the polls, as well as one that requires time and, sometimes, skills, and one that demands money. Still, these activities comprise only a small subset of the types of participatory acts that fit under the definition we introduced in Section 1.1. To compensate, we undertook additional analyses using data from study years (2016 and 2020) that included questions about other forms of participation–protesting, contacting public officials, and being active on local issues. We present these results in Appendix O.[14] Our larger story about the causes of the gender gap and its closing over time remains consistent when we are able to include these additional political activities. With respect to contributions to political campaigns, the ANES asks only whether respondents made a donation but not about its size, which can vary substantially. In Section 5, when we take up gender differences in donating to political campaigns in greater detail, we supplement our analysis with data from OpenSecrets.com about top-dollar donors in presidential election years. We note that the ANES does not include more complex measures of gender beyond the binary of "women" and "men," so we limit our analysis to these groups.

We have a further caveat about the data we employ. The ANES likely overestimates rates of political participation. We know that this bias pertains to reported voting, as researchers have compared the ANES turnout rates to other reputable surveys and to official voter rolls and have noted a persistent gap.[15] Jackman and Spahn (2019) attribute the majority of the overestimation in the ANES to two factors. First, the randomly selected individuals who then choose to participate in the surveys are more likely to be politically active than those who decline to participate. Second, participating in the ANES itself serves as a mobilizing force; individuals who take part in the study are stimulated to participate at higher rates than we otherwise would observe. The remaining overestimation is due to social desirability bias. Study participants want to appear as good citizens who engage in desirable behaviors and may erroneously report having registered and voted.[16]

---

[14] Although some assume the gender gap in activity is reversed for such political acts, the reality is complicated (Burns, Schlozman, and Verba 2001, chap. 3).

[15] The overestimation may vary from year to year. Jackman and Spahn (2019) suggest that, at least in 2012, ANES turnout rates were biased by 13–19 percentage points.

[16] Jenkins et al. (2021) find race-related social desirability bias likely to inflate the reported participation of Black survey respondents to the ANES, particularly when the interviewers are also Black.

To compensate for overreporting voting behavior due to social desirability bias, some researchers propose that any analysis include only those ANES survey respondents whose voting behavior has been validated by comparing their reported behavior to official government records. Research on voter validation, however, provides good reasons not to pursue this strategy. For one, survey respondents' self-reported behavior is, in fact, relatively accurate (Berent, Krosnick, and Lupia 2016). Indeed, in their study of the ANES overestimation problem, Jackman and Spahn find that false reporting accounts for only 6 percent of the bias. Second, while validated vote data often suggest lower turnout rates than self-reported data, that "lower turnout" picture is not necessarily more accurate. It is simply a version of turnout with different biases than are present in self-reports with a good sampling frame (see, e.g., Traugott and Katosh 1979; Presser and Traugott 1992; McDonald 2007; Berent, Krosnick, and Lupia 2016).

While we acknowledge that the overall rates of participation as reported by the ANES may be somewhat inflated compared to the true rates in the U.S. population, we are less interested in exact levels of participation than in the disparity in participation between men and women. We have less reason to suspect that the overestimation biases in the ANES bear on the differences between men and women.[17] We should also point out that our focus on the reversal of the gender gap in voting and the narrowing of the gender gap in other forms of participation means that the biases inherent in our main source of evidence are likely to yield findings that are conservative estimates. To allay potential concerns, we provide further discussion of ANES turnout rates in Appendix A.

We should also note that ANES data limit our ability to investigate two factors we know to be associated with political participation: civic skills and requests for activity (Verba, Schlozman, and Brady 1995; Burns, Schlozman, and Verba 2001). Civic skills are the organizational and communications capacities developed over the life course – including in such adult nonpolitical domains as the workplace, nonpolitical organizations, and religious institutions – that make it easier to take part in politics. Those who, for example, organize meetings and make presentations on the job or in a fraternal organization are more likely to be politically active. Unfortunately, the ANES does not have a consistent battery of civic skills questions.

In addition, those who are asked to become politically active are much more likely to do so. The relationship between being targeted by a request to participate

---

[17] Some prior work, however, suggests men are more likely than women to overreport voting (Traugott and Katosh 1979; more recently, Stockemer and Sundstrom 2023). In some years, women's voting deficit thus may be overestimated.

and actually taking part is complex (Schlozman, Brady, and Verba, 2018, chap. 7). Respondents in surveys indicate that requests for participation are often successful in generating political activity that might not have taken place. However, those who seek to mobilize political activity target their requests at people with attributes suggesting that they would be likely to say yes and to participate effectively when they take part – by, for example, writing a compelling letter or making a large political donation. The upshot of these processes of activation is that requests beget political activity, and past activity begets requests.[18]

We should recognize important limitations to the analyses we can conduct across subgroups. In many earlier years of the ANES time series, there are insufficient Black and Hispanic respondents for reliable analysis (weighted sample sizes for all groups across the ANES years analyzed are available in Appendix B). In 2008 and 2012, however, the ANES oversampled Black and Hispanic Americans, yielding large enough samples for investigation of gender differences in participation among these groups. Furthermore, in each survey year from 2012 to 2020, the ANES also conducted online companion surveys to the usual face-to-face interviews. We combine the two survey modes in these years to achieve larger samples. We are committed to investigating and presenting intersectional race-gender analyses, but we proceed with the caveat that the variability in the data for Black and Hispanic respondents may limit our ability to draw confident conclusions to the answers we seek for race-gender subgroups. When possible, we replicated our results with data from the National Politics Study in 2004 and 2008 (which has a representative sample of Black Americans), the results of which are available in Appendix H.

While many of the issues with sample size result from trying to study subgroups within a nationally representative sample, it is also worth stressing that this statistical difficulty speaks to a set of enduring realities in the larger population that certainly reduce the political activity of these subgroups, and therefore voice and equality. In particular, the numbers of Black and Hispanic men are reduced in these datasets (and the larger voting population) for reasons of disproportionate incarceration and higher mortality rates than other subgroups (Wolfers, Quealy, and Leonhardt 2015). The disproportionate rate of

---

[18] Although the ANES does not contain the multiple items that permit us to delineate in detail who asked whom to do what, it has long contained a question about party contacting that asks, in part: "Did anyone from one of the political parties call you up or come round to talk to you about the campaign this year?" Importantly, this question has been asked in the same way for decades (although political communications now come in other forms, such as texts or emails). When we add this measure of party contacting to our multivariate analyses, it is significantly related to participation for both men and women. And, although having been contacted by a party is related to education, both party contact and education are significant, again, for women and for men. Results of these analyses and full question wording are in Appendix F.

incarceration among Black men in the United States bears on our analysis. The ANES data do not include institutionalized members of the population. Pettit (2012) points out that ignoring the incarcerated results in the inflation of estimated voter turnout rates among Black men, which distorts the portrait of the gender gap in participation we paint for Black Americans. Nonetheless, we do our best, using some of the best tools available, to understand cross-racial and ethnic group differences with regard to gender and participation.

An additional challenge is that, over time, the composition of the overall population and the intersectional groups within it changes. For example, with respect to the complicated matter of incarceration, the period of our study saw a sharp rise in rates of incarceration and felon disenfranchisement, developments with disproportionate consequences for the representation of Black men in the electorate (Uggen et al. 2022). Another example is the substantial growth in the share of the U.S. population that is of Hispanic origin since the 1970s. Moreover, recent Hispanic immigrants are relatively less likely to come from Mexico than in the past and relatively more likely to originate from the Caribbean, Central America, or South America, with implications for the distribution of nationalities and, therefore, group identity among Hispanic Americans. Unfortunately, our data often do not permit us to delve into these kinds of developments. Still, it is useful to recall that, while such categories as race and gender are central to our analysis, they are neither monolithic nor necessarily stable.

2.2 Models of Political Participation

Much of the analysis to come entails examining the factors that predict political participation separately for men and women. We hope to locate the roots of the diminishing gender gap in political participation in processes such that some of these factors are changing in ways that are different for women than they are for men. Our main analytical tool is multiple regression, which allows us to model political participation as a function of key factors that have been found in the past to explain changes in participation while holding constant other relevant predictors of political activity.[19] In particular, we run these regressions separately for men and women as groups, or for gendered racial and ethnic subgroups, allowing these factors to matter or vary differently (Burns, Schlozman, and Verba 2001). This approach allows us to isolate the effect of a particular

---

[19] For ease of interpretation and consistency, we employ ordinary least squares regression analysis, even though many of our outcome variables are binary. Prior work shows that OLS yields similar results to logistic regression estimates (Hellevik 2009). We have, however, replicated our analysis with other estimators where appropriate and have confirmed that our substantive conclusions are the same (analysis available upon request).

explanatory variable while taking into account other potentially causal or confounding factors.

For dependent variables we focus on three forms of political participation: voting, campaign participation, and donating to political campaigns. To estimate changes in these variables, we build models that include what earlier research has shown to be fundamental predictors of participation: education, income, and political interest. We also consider the possibility that the presence of women in visible positions in the political environment influences women's political engagement.

Education is related to almost every other factor found to foster participation. For example, those with high levels of education are more likely to be interested in and informed about politics. They have higher incomes. They are more likely to command organizational and communications skills that facilitate political involvement and to be in jobs, networks, and institutional settings where they will be targeted by requests to where they will be targeted by requests for political activity.[20] Therefore, our empirical models include both education (measured in seven categories including grade school, high school [no diploma], high school [diploma], high school [diploma and non-academic training], some college or associates degree, college, or advanced degree) and family income (measured in five groups).

Individuals vary in how interested they are in politics. A general interest in the political world tends to be strongly associated with political participation. A long line of research has found notable gender differences in levels of political interest, with men generally being more interested in politics than women (Prior 2018 provides a review). Thus, we include in our model a measure of interest based on respondents' answers to a question about how interested they were in the political campaigns in the year in which they were surveyed.

To examine the effects of women candidates in the political environment, we created the *Composition of the Political Environment (CPE) Database*, in which we coded, for the years 2008–2020, a variety of characteristics, including the party, gender, and race or ethnicity, of incumbents and general-election candidates for the offices of governor, U.S. House, and U.S. Senate. In order to assess potential relationships between a respondent's political participation and the characteristics of politicians in the immediate environment, we linked these data to the individual respondents surveyed in ANES by state and congressional district.

As previous research (Burns, Schlozman, and Verba 2001, chap. 8) finds that both paid work and activity within religious institutions facilitate political participation by inculcating civic skills and providing exposure to requests for

---

[20] On the association between educational attainment and political participation, see the alternative perspectives in Verba, Schlozman, and Brady (1995, chap. 15), Nie, Junn, and Stehlik-Barry (1996), Kam and Palmer (2008), and Berinsky and Lenz (2011).

political activity, our models include controls for employment status and church attendance. We also account for marital status (whether or not the respondent is married) and age, with an additional variable indicating whether the respondent is over sixty-five. Earlier work finds that married individuals are more likely to participate in politics, perhaps because marriage provides social and economic stability (Wolfinger and Rosenstone 1980; Wolfinger and Wolfinger 2008). In addition, married people have other unmeasured characteristics – for example, they are more likely to own their homes – associated with political activity. Previous scholarship has shown the relationship between age and participation to be curvilinear: young adults start out as relatively inactive; participation rises before peaking in middle age and then drops off with very old age. According to one analysis (Schlozman, Verba, and Brady 2012, chap. 8), this pattern can be partially explained by age-related differences in nearly all the attributes related to political activity – for example, income, civic skills, and political interest. In the multivariate analyses to come, all variables have been rescaled to range from zero to one, for ease of comprehension and comparison.

In sum, for each presidential year between 1964 and 2020, we will estimate, separately for men and women, and then further separately for subgroups defined by both gender and race or ethnicity, models of the three forms of participation with these explanatory variables. Our goal is to identify the degree to which any of the factors have had a marked influence on the closing, and, in some cases, the reversal, of gaps in participation between men and women. We know that our model specification is not exhaustive. Additional factors can lead individuals to participate, although we suspect none supplant the effects of the factors included in our estimations. Our more parsimonious models allow us to assess over time how key factors affect the gender gap in political activity.

2.3 Two Approaches to Studying Changes in Participation: Levels and Effects

We consider the major factors shaping changes in the gender gap in participation from two perspectives. In our exploration of the roots of the narrowing of the gender gap in political activity, we assess changes over time in both the *relative amounts (levels)* of any particular participatory factor commanded by women and men and the *relative impacts (effects)* of those factors on participation. As an example of the differences between levels and effects, consider the fact that women who work full-time, year-round, have long earned less than men. Among the multiple explanations for this outcome are that, in the past, women were not, on average, as well educated as men in the work force (level); additionally, at each rung on the educational ladder, women were, on average, less able than men to turn their education into earnings (effect). We consider education and income similarly in this analysis.

Regarding the relative *levels* of the factors associated with participation, we consider how much, on average, of any particular participatory factor women command relative to men. What matters for changing disparities in participation between women and men is not simply whether there are significant gender differences in average education, income, or political interest, but how those gaps are changing in relative terms. For example, it is well known that men have higher average incomes than women. If women begin to catch up, then the gender gap in participation would narrow a bit – even if men's incomes remain higher, on average, than women's.

Thinking about *effects* is another story. What is consequential for the narrowing of the gender gap in participation there is how the impact of particular participatory factors may change for men and women, in relative terms. To pose a hypothetical, let us suppose that the coefficient on education for political participation is significantly higher for men than for women, indicating an advantage for men in the participatory payoff from gains in education. Regardless of the levels – in this case, how much education men or women command – any particular level of educational attainment would, for men, be associated with significantly greater participation. Now let us suppose that over time, the gender difference in the effects of education on participation were to disappear – either because the effect for women became stronger or because the effect for men became weaker. The net result would be that, over time, the gender gap in political participation would diminish – even if women made no relative gain in their average amount of education.

For those particular about causal inference, we admittedly use the term "effect" somewhat loosely. One limitation of our analytical approach is that we cannot in fact fully identify causal effects, only associations between variables. Nevertheless, we use the term "effect" interchangeably with the term "association" to describe relationships among variables. In subsequent sections, we return to the distinction between levels and effects and explain it further within the context of our study of the gender gap in participation.[21]

2.4 What Influences Participation?

As we proceed, we use the techniques just described to consider alternative solutions to the puzzle of the closing (and, in some cases, reversal) of the gender

---

[21] We checked our inferences using models with interaction terms. Those interactive models yielded the same results as the easier-to-read models we present here.

disparity in participation. We use our initial multivariate regression results, focusing on all women and all men, to guide our interest in both resources and politics (each of which gets its own set of analyses in major sections subsequently). As shown in Table 1, among the factors we explore, the two most consistent predictors of voting, campaign participation, and donating are education and electoral interest, with income a close third. That is, even holding constant many other factors, higher levels of educational attainment, electoral interest, and income are associated with an enhanced likelihood of individuals taking part in these activities (see Appendix D for full models).

2.5 Summary

In this section, we highlighted the utility of the ANES for undertaking these longitudinal analyses. We also described the basic model of participation we use to estimate the relationship between various political and social factors and three forms of electoral activity: voting, campaign participation, and donating. As discussed, our empirical strategy involves considering not only how the ingredients of participation have changed over time, but also how shifts in relative levels of the different factors may have affected the gender gap in participation, and whether our results for all men and women vary by racial and ethnic subgroups.

In our search for an explanation for why the gender gap in political participation closed we pursue two lines of inquiry. In Section 3, we investigate whether something changed in the political environment that affected differentially women's and men's propensities to take part. In Section 4, we explore the possibility that some social-structural shift altered the relative balance of participatory resources between women and men – most likely involving such socioeconomic factors as education or income – and, thus, had an impact on the gender disparity in participation.

3 What about Politics?

Political participation is, of course, intimately connected to the political environment that fosters or inhibits it. Any number of aspects of the political environment – ranging from electoral laws to social movements to candidates and issues – have potential consequences for participation. In this section, we consider the role of the electoral environment on the gender gap in political activity. We begin with a brief look at how proximate political circumstances might influence the political participation of women and men. We focus at greater length on a longer-term development – the changing gender composition of the set of politicians who contest and hold visible public office – and ask

Table 1 Predictors of participation among women and men, 1976–2020

Women

Year	1976	1980	1984	1988	1992	1996	2000	2004	2008	2012	2016	2020
Voting	Education *Income* Interest	Education Interest	Education Income Interest	Education Income Interest	Education Income Interest	Education *Income* Interest	Education Income Interest	Education Income Interest	Education *Income* Interest	Education Income Interest	Education Income Interest	Education Income Interest
Campaign	Education Interest	*Education* Interest	Education Interest	Education Interest	Education Interest	Education Interest	Education Interest	Education Interest	Education Interest	Education Interest	Education Interest	Education Interest
Donating	Education *Income* Interest	Education Income Interest	Education Income Interest	Education Income Interest	Education Income Interest	Education Interest	Income Interest	Education Interest	Education Income Interest	Education Income Interest	Education Income Interest	Education Income Interest

Men

Year	1976	1980	1984	1988	1992	1996	2000	2004	2008	2012	2016	2020
Voting	Education Income Interest	Interest	Education Income Interest	Education Income Interest	Education Income Interest	Education Income Interest	Education *Income* Interest	Education Income Interest	Education Interest	Education Interest	*Education* *Income* Interest	Education Income Interest
Campaign	Education Income *Interest*	Interest	Interest	Education Income Interest	Education Interest	Interest	Interest	*Education* Interest	*Interest*	*Education* Interest	Income Interest	Education Interest
Donating	Education Income Interest	Income Interest	Education Income Interest	Education Income Interest	Education Income Interest	Education Income Interest	Education Income Interest	*Education* Income interest	Education	Education Interest	Income Interest	Education *Income* Interest

Note: For each year, Table 1 indicates whether there is a statistically significant association between any of the primary independent variables (education, income, electoral interest) and one of the primary dependent variables in our regression models (voting, campaign participation, or donating). We only list the significant factors in the table. Where the font is italicized, the association is significant at the .1 level; otherwise, the association is significant at the .05 level.

Source: Data from the ANES cumulative file and the 2020 ANES (weighted).

whether women's political activity as citizens increases as more women have run for office and served in government.

3.1 Proximate Political Circumstances and the Gender Gap in Participation

The ongoing battles over reproductive rights, the defeat of the Equal Rights Amendment, and the #MeToo movement are only a few examples of the extent to which concerns about gender have been salient to our politics in recent decades. The millions of hand-sewn "pink pussy hats" worn by women marching the day after Donald Trump's inauguration in early 2017, a protest characterized as "likely the largest single-day demonstration in recorded U.S. history" (Chenoweth and Pressman 2017), serve as a visible reminder of the mobilizing potential of immediate political events.

Recent elections show that proximate political events can have participatory consequences for particular publics. Figure 4 presents a striking example. When Barack Obama was on the ballot in 2008 and 2012, campaign participation among Black Americans increased sharply (Philpot, Shaw, and McGowen 2009; Clark 2014; Kinder and Chudy 2016). In contrast, the 2016 election, the first election in U.S. history with a woman as the presidential candidate of a major party, was not characterized by exceptional campaign activity by women, even with the exceptional gender focus of the electoral environment.

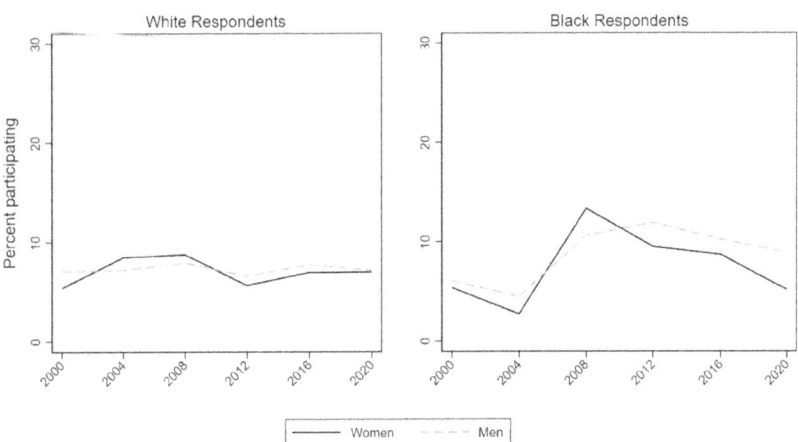

Figure 4 Percent of white and Black respondents participating in campaign activities* by gender: 2000–2020

Data from the ANES cumulative file and the 2020 ANES (weighted). The gender differences are not statistically significant in any year.

* Includes attending a political meeting or rally or working for a candidate.

Neither Hillary Clinton, the first woman to achieve a major-party presidential nomination, nor Donald Trump, the candidate of aggrieved masculinity,[22] generated particularly high levels of political participation.

That Clinton's groundbreaking candidacy seems not to have inspired a spike in overall turnout or a boost to women's participation relative to men's is our first indication that changes in the gendered nature of individual campaigns may not explain the closing of the gender gap. Neither the historic 2016 election nor the subsequent one in 2020 when Kamala Harris ran successfully for vice president seems to have had a meaningful impact on the gender gap in participation. If these major historic events did not produce a surge in participation, what about the less newsworthy long-term expansion in women's presence in politics? Has the slow-moving, but ultimately substantial, shift in women's presence in the political environment contributed to the closing of the gender gap in participation?

3.2 A Longer-Term Change: The Gender Composition of the Political Environment

The last several decades have witnessed an ongoing transformation in the gender composition of the political environment with possible implications for the gender gap in political participation. Women have entered politics and occupy visible positions at rates very different from what prevailed at the beginning of our time series in the 1970s. Figure 5 shows the steady upward trend in the proportion of women among state legislators and members of the U.S. House and Senate. The figure also reveals an increase in women governors over time, but the somewhat more dramatic slope shifts in the trend line reflect the relatively smaller number of women governors.

As of late 2024, very few Black or Hispanic women have ever served in either the U.S. Senate or governors' mansions. Only three Black women have ever been U.S. senators – Carol Moseley Braun, Kamala Harris, and Laphonza Butler – and none has been a governor. New Mexico is the only state that has ever had a Latina governor – Susana Martinez in 2011, followed by Michelle Lujan Grisham in 2017. Nevada is the only state that has ever had a Latina senator: Catherine Cortez Masto.

In view of these small numbers, when it comes to race and ethnicity, we focus on the U.S. House. Figure 6, which presents data about the U.S. House, contains numbers that are more encouraging. Black and Hispanic women have made

---

[22] On Trump's aggrieved masculinity and misogyny and their consequences, see, among many others, Dittmar (2016); Maxwell and Shields (2017); Shear and Sullivan (2018); Boatright and Sperling (2020); and the video compilation of Trump's demeaning comments about women at www.youtube.com/watch?v=-55hPvPnTOU.

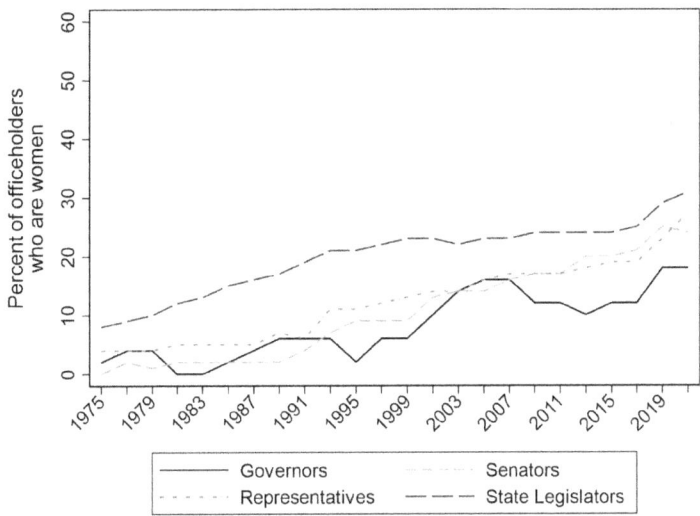

Figure 5 Percent of U.S. officeholders at different levels who are women: 1975–2021

Data from the Center for American Women and Politics (CAWP 2023c) and the Composition in the Political Environment (CPE) Database (collected by authors).

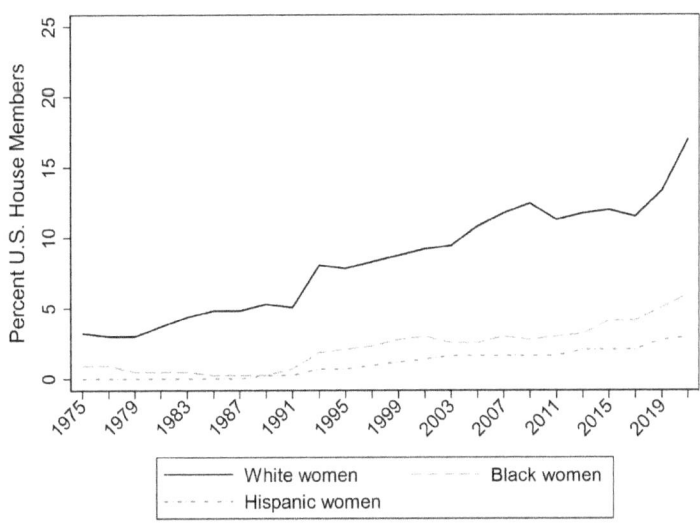

Figure 6 Share of women in the U.S. House by gender and race or ethnicity: 1975–2021

Data from the Center for American Women and Politics (CAWP 2023c) and the CPE Database (collected by authors).

strides such that Black women currently constitute 6 percent and Hispanic women 4 percent of the members of the U.S. House (Dittmar 2021 and Dittmar 2022).

Figure 7 displays the percent of U.S. citizens represented by a woman in at least one of the following roles: governor, senator, or member of Congress. The natural consequence of the steady increase of women in office is a corresponding increase in the share of members of the public who are represented by a woman.[23] In 1975, just over 5 percent of the population was

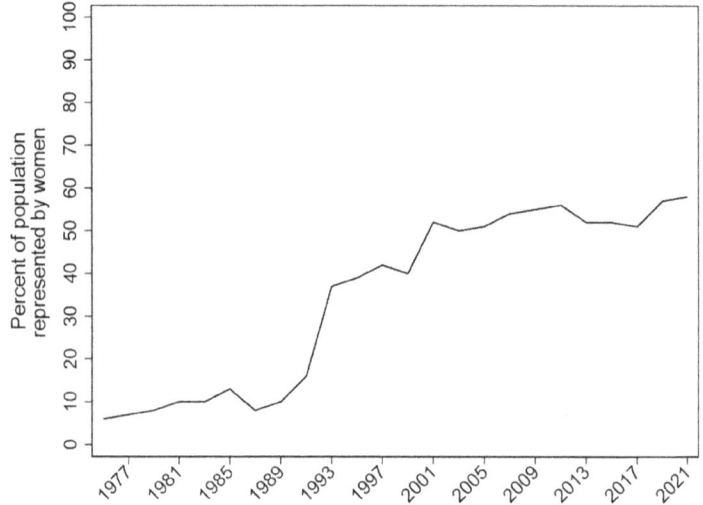

Figure 7 Percent of U.S. citizens represented by at least one visible female elected official: 1975–2021

Calculations based on the CPE Database (collected by authors) and U.S. Census Bureau and other population data matched to congressional districts. Women representatives include governors, U.S. Senators, or members of the U.S. House of Representatives.

---

[23] The data in Figure 7 were collected with the assistance of undergraduates at Boston and Harvard Colleges who are thanked in the acknowledgments. We used data about state populations from the U.S. Census and information about elected officials from the *Almanac of American Politics* to calculate the proportion of the public that is represented by a woman in the U.S House, Senate, or governor's mansion. For any state (except for very small ones, for which we used the actual population of congressional districts) with at least one female representative in the House but neither a woman governor nor a woman senator, we assumed that each congressional District represents 1/435th of the nation. We were concerned to assess whether this assumption introduced error – especially late in any decade. Uneven population growth means that congressional districts that were of roughly equal size just after a reapportionment might differ substantially in size as that reapportionment becomes more distant. We checked by coding the data for 2019 two ways, first using the 1/435th assumption, and then using figures for actual populations of congressional districts. The results were nearly identical.

represented by a woman in one of these visible offices – rising to over 52 percent by the beginning of this century, and 58 percent in 2021. A dramatic change was produced by the elections of 1992, the Year of the Woman. In 1991, only 16 percent of the U.S. population was represented by a woman in a visible public office. Two years later, the figure had more than doubled to 37 percent. By the first decade of the 2000s this trend slowed. One plausible explanation for this plateau is that many of the same districts may have continued to elect women over time – in particular, districts that are more urban, more liberal, and higher in SES are especially likely to elect and reelect women. Palmer and Simon 2006 call these "women-friendly districts" (see also Ondercin 2022). Politicians, male and female, are strategic about running in districts they have a higher likelihood of winning. Therefore, in some cases, women elected to these visible offices replace other women.

3.3 Does the Gender Composition of the Immediate Political Environment Make a Difference?

Is the recent narrowing of the disparity between women and men in political activity that we documented in Section 1 related to the increased representation of women among public officials? One way to think about this question is to consider gender congruence in political representation. Does being in an environment where there are women contesting and holding visible public offices have consequences for the political activity of women as citizens? What about for men? It turns out that gender congruence for men is nearly universal. That is, with rare exceptions, men in the United States consistently have at least one male visible public official (governor, senator, or member of Congress). The exceptions, the first of which occurred in some congressional districts in Washington in 2005, have never constituted as much as 1 percent of the population.

In view of this circumstance, the question becomes whether living in an environment in which there are women contesting and holding visible elected office has an impact on the size of the gender gap in political activity by virtue of a differential effect on women's and men's participation. Others have tackled this question with mixed results.[24] Previous studies differ from one another on a number of dimensions. One area of variation is which dependent variables are

---

[24] See, for example, Lawless 2004; Campbell and Wolbrecht 2006; Dolan 2006; Atkeson and Carrillo 2007; Beaman et al. 2012; Cassese, Bos, and Schneider 2014; Lawless and Fox 2015; Shames 2015; Wolak 2015; Shames 2017; Wolbrecht and Campbell 2017; Cassese and Holman 2019; Clayton, O'Brien, and Piscopo 2019; Oliver and Conroy 2020; Thomsen and King 2020; Bos et al. 2022. As Campbell and Wolbrecht (2025) put it: "the degree to which women politicians are in fact role models remains very much open to debate, with findings often described as mixed or weak ... and others reporting no effects at all."

included in the analysis: psychological orientations to politics such as electoral interest, engagement, or efficacy; political discussion; political participation. Another is the measure of exposure: candidates or officeholders or both; the proportion of women in U.S. House or the state legislature or a dyadic relationship such that the respondent is represented by a woman in the geographically defined constituency; media coverage of visible political women. Still another is the age of the respondents: adults or adolescents. And yet another is when the research was conducted. Amid the inconsistent findings, it is difficult to discern patterns of the circumstances under which the political environment is or is not associated with enhanced political involvement for women.

A notable body of research has also considered the effect of Black and Hispanic elected leaders on participation among Black and Hispanic citizens. For example, Bobo and Gilliam (1990) find evidence that Black Americans living in or in proximity to cities with Black mayors experience greater political efficacy and participate at higher rates than those who do not live in "high empowerment" areas. Tate's (2004) study of the effects of Black members of Congress on Black Americans' political engagement yields similar results (although see Gay 2001). Building on this work, we consider whether candidate congruence with respect to race *and* gender influences political participation.

Discerning a gender difference in the effect of the gender composition does not necessarily reveal the mechanism behind it. We can, however, suggest several possible alternatives. One possibility involves cues and role modeling – women exposed to changes in the gender composition of their immediate political environment getting the implicit message that politics is not just a man's game (Verba, Burns, and Schlozman 1997; Burns, Schlozman, and Verba 2001, chap. 13). Another is selective political mobilization – whether originating in campaigns for women candidates or in social media and other networks – that has the intent or effect of disproportionately energizing women, or subgroups of women, to take part. Still another is a selection effect such that the places where women seek or gain office are, in some way, systematically different (Hinojosa 2012, Ondercin 2022).[25] Whatever the mechanism that might produce such a selective boost to women's activity, the phenomenon we are investigating is anchored geographically in states or congressional districts, and so relates to the relationship of representation between the public official and the particular geographical constituency. It would, thus, not be equivalent to any potential nationwide impact of the multiple developments in Washington that have injected gender into national politics in recent years.

---

[25] For a helpful review of potential mechanisms, see Hinojosa and Kittilson (2020) on the difference between viability and visibility and on the contrast between small changes in descriptive representation as compared with larger changes in politics, for example, the Year of the Woman.

With regard to the consequences of the gender composition of the political environment, across the whole population and within groups defined by race and ethnicity, men and women are for the most part similarly distributed throughout the United States and across electoral districts. Thus, there is no gender difference regarding the *level* of women in the political environment. However, it is possible that men and women experience these political environments differently. Any impact on the gender gap in political activity of exposure to women in visible political positions must, therefore, derive from a gender difference in *effects*.

In Figure 8 we present the results of an analysis in which we consider the *effect* on voting, campaign participation, and donating of the presence of women in the political environment – defined as a female governor, member of the U.S. Senate or House, or a successful candidate for one of these offices.[26] Each part of Figure 8 shows, for a particular form of political activity, the regression coefficients by election year, holding constant the other factors – for example, educational attainment and marital status – discussed in Section 2. Contrary to the reasonable expectation that having one or more women holding or contesting visible public office might have a positive influence on participation, we find no direct, significant impact on any of three forms of engagement for women – or, for that matter, men. In fact, in no case is there a significant and consistent gender difference in the effect of women candidates or officeholders (Appendix D presents the results for both men and women). Out of thirty-six models predicting participation, the only time the presence of women candidates achieves statistical significance is for donating to a political campaign in 1996. In short, the search for a direct effect of the presence of visible women in the electoral environment on voting, campaign participation, or donating produces disappointing results.[27]

---

[26] We do not consider a losing female candidate for one of these offices as a visible woman in the immediate political environment. This subjective choice is intended to be a conservative approach to the data analysis; it is likely that a woman running for governor or U.S. senate within a state would indeed be visible, even if her candidacy is unsuccessful, but we prefer to make the analysis a hard test. We also err on the side of caution as senatorial and gubernatorial candidates make up a relatively small portion of our dataset and the large portion consists of candidates for the U.S. House, and a losing congressional female candidate is unlikely to have been "visible" in the same way.

[27] In Section 3.6, we explore the possibility that the presence of women candidates is non-randomly assigned – that is, that higher electoral interest among women or among some groups of women may drive more women candidates to emerge. One might also wonder whether the clustering of cases (see Section P in the appendix for a portrait of the distribution of cases) means we estimate standard errors that are too small for coefficients on the variables about the presence of women candidates. Were we to find a string of systematic effects, we could re-estimate our models as multi-level models to be sure that we are not overstating our certainty. We do not, in fact, find systematic effects. Sometimes scholars control for a series of characteristics of districts to ensure that the effect is appropriately attributed to the presence of women candidates (Burns, Schlozman, and Verba 2001, pp. 347–348; Campbell and Wolbrecht 2025), but those controls have made no difference to the estimated coefficient of interest, and so we do not pursue that strategy here.

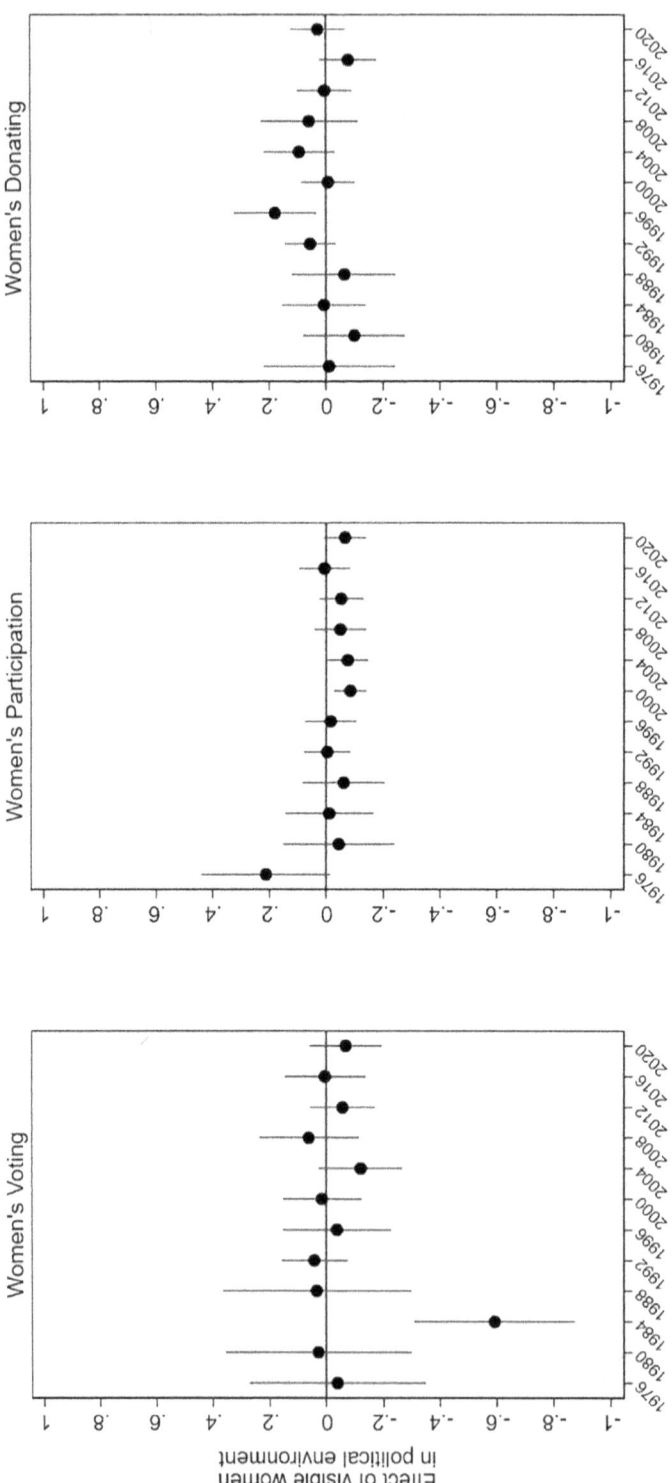

Figure 8 Effect of visible women in political environment on women's political participation: 1976–2020
Data from the ANES cumulative file and the 2020 ANES (weighted) and the authors' CPE Database.

3.4 Party, Race or Ethnicity, and Gender in the Political Environment: Does Closer Congruence Increase Participation?

Because women and men are further divided by party, race, ethnicity, and other identities, attributes, and beliefs, not all women will see all female candidates as potential descriptive representatives (Sanbonmatsu 2006; Klar 2018; Elder 2021; Lemi 2021). It may be that the gender congruence that would mobilize participation would be among copartisans or within racial or ethnic groups. We focus first on partisanship, entertaining the possibility that congruence with *both* party and gender is important for participation. Then, we turn our attention to congruence with both gender and race or ethnicity.

It is plausible that the gender composition of the political environment would have an impact only if there were partisan correspondence. To a Republican woman, a Democratic woman contesting or holding visible office – or, conversely, to a Democratic woman, a Republican woman contesting or holding visible office – might not function to mobilize political action. In fact, it might discourage such participation. When we separate respondents by both gender and party, we find – nothing. Of 144 coefficients (3 participatory acts for Republican and Democratic women and men across 12 electoral cycles), only 3 are positive and significant for women, and 2 are positive and significant for men. Even when we group the congruent analyses (combining Republican-congruent and Democratic congruent women and those contesting or holding office), only 5 of 36 become significant and 7 of 36 are significant for men (see Appendix L). In sum, even when there is partisan congruence, the presence of women in the political environment does not activate political participation for women in either major party.

As for the congruence between visible public figures and individual citizens in terms of race or ethnicity as well as gender, we focus as usual on six subgroups: women and men who are Hispanic, Black, and white. Earlier research theorizes that candidate congruence with respect to race or ethnicity can be politically empowering and mobilizing, a claim that has empirical evidence to support it – at least in part because Black and Hispanic candidates have been relatively rare in comparison to the number of white candidates.[28] The novelty of Black and Hispanic candidates, coupled with the long-standing deficit in symbolic political representation of these groups, provides good reason to anticipate a mobilizing effect for citizens from these ethno-racial groups when candidates who look like them run for office. We do not necessarily have the same expectations for racial congruence among whites or

---

[28] See Browning, Marshall, and Tabb (1984, 1986); Bobo and Gilliam (1990); de la Garza and DeSipio (1993); Tate (1993); Shaw, de la Garza, and Lee (2000); Pantoja, Ramirez, and Segura (2001); Barreto, Segura, and Woods (2004); Griffin and Keane (2006); Washington (2006); Barreto (2007, 2010); Whitby (2007); Rocha et al. (2010); and Fraga (2018).

gender congruence among men, for the very reasons we just laid out (although see Gay 2002). And again, the political environment would not sustain such an analysis; all white respondents in the ANES – regardless of gender – were exposed to at least one visible white political figure in the immediate environment of their state or congressional district. All men – regardless of race or ethnicity – had at least one man among the visible political figures in their immediate political environment.

While men and women are nearly equal in number and evenly distributed within states and congressional districts, white, Black, or Hispanic Americans are groups of varying sizes, and they are distributed unevenly across jurisdictions. For example, nearly two in five residents of Mississippi – but only 1 percent of those in Montana – are Black. Half the residents of New Mexico, but 2 percent of those in West Virginia, are Hispanic (U.S. Census Bureau 2024). To compound the complexities, the representation of these racial and ethnic groups within the American population has changed across the period we examine. Since the 1970s, Americans have become more likely to be Hispanic and less likely to be non-Hispanic white. Taken together, these considerations imply that, in contrast to our analysis of the impact of having a visible woman in the immediate political environment for women and for men, levels vary across the six groups defined by both gender and race or ethnicity. Therefore, we will be sensitive to both levels and effects.

As usual, we rely on the ANES. Because the ANES employs a cluster sample approach to produce a nationally representative sample, it does not draw Black and Hispanic male and female respondents from every congressional district in the United States. Thus, the survey yields race-gender matched respondents for most but not all congressional districts with a candidate or public official who is Black or Hispanic. Our checks, found in Appendix P, indicate that our data coverage was good but not fully complete. Furthermore, because of the cluster sampling strategy and the limited number of Black and Hispanic respondents in the ANES samples, the numbers of cases are sometimes quite small for some of the relevant groups. To compensate, we merged the data for the four surveys conducted in the presidential election years from 2008 through 2020 (and included year fixed effects in all multivariate analyses).

For data about the gender and race or ethnicity of both candidates and elected officials, we drew on several sources to build an original data set. Gary Jacobson generously shared his longitudinal data about congressional elections. We also took advantage of the data assembled by Bernard L. Fraga and Hans Hassell on the demographics of congressional candidates through 2014. The website of the Center for American Women and Politics at Rutgers University lists every woman who has served as a governor, senator, or member of the House. In addition, we generated our own data using searches of Ballotpedia, *Almanac of American Politics*, and the CQ Voting and Elections Collection.[29]

Our earlier observation about the mobilizing impact of the Obama candidacy led us to expect that racial or ethnic congruence would have a powerful effect on participation. We note, however, that the evidence for the effect of co-racial or co-ethnic candidates on participation has been mixed (Gay 2001; Keele and White 2011; Henderson, Sekhon, and Titiunik 2016; Fraga 2018). We tested the effect of racial or ethnic congruence, gender congruence, race-gender congruence, and the effect of racial or ethnic congruent women in the political environment for each of three dependent variables and six groups. We generated many results (Appendix J), and yet our findings do not demonstrate a definitive trend in the relationship between identity-congruent members of the political environment and political participation.

Significant findings are infrequent and do not fall into any coherent pattern. We do find that white women are more likely to go to the polls if there is a visible woman in the political environment – regardless of her race or ethnicity. Black women are somewhat more likely to engage in campaign participation when the political environment includes a visible Black politician regardless of gender.

Moreover, the findings for making political contributions are downright confusing. White women are somewhat more likely to donate, and white men even more likely to donate, when there is a white woman in the immediate political environment. Black men are somewhat more likely to contribute when there is a Black man in the immediate political environment. However, Hispanic women are significantly less likely to make a donation when the immediate political environment includes a visible Hispanic winner or incumbent, whether a woman or a man. And Black and Hispanic men are significantly less likely to contribute when the political environment includes a visible woman sharing his race or ethnicity. Overall, we cannot conclude that correspondence on the basis of gender plus race or ethnicity consistently boosts political activity.

3.5 A Matter of Interest

Our earlier work (Burns, Schlozman, and Verba 2001, chap. 13) also showed no direct association between the gender composition of the political environment and political activity for either women or men. However, we did find that,

---

[29] When these sources did not contain sufficient information to code race or ethnicity, we did not rely exclusively on photographs or names but instead conducted extensive searches of campaign websites and social media, news media, and any other relevant and reputable online sources. In compiling this dataset, we relied heavily on the work of undergraduate assistants, who are thanked in the Acknowledgments. Further information about dataset construction, variables, and choices is in Appendix C.

during the 1990s, the presence of women contesting and holding visible office had an indirect impact on women's participation, *through political interest*, a finding confirmed in Campbell and Wolbrecht (2025). This effect, which disappeared in the 2000s (Burns et al. 2018), was not apparent for men. Exposure to visible women in the immediate political environment seemed to increase women's, but not men's, political interest and knowledge with the downstream consequence of enhancing their participation. The bottom line was a suggestion that gender equality in the contesting and holding of visible public office could reduce the gender gap in participation – even without increasing women's access to other participatory resources.

Not unexpectedly, people who are interested in politics are also more likely to take part in politics. Echoing what we saw in Table 1, Figure 9 shows that, for women, electoral interest has a consistently positive and statistically significant relationship to campaign participation. The effect for men (not pictured) is quite similar.

In view of the association between electoral interest and campaign participation, we investigated whether the gender composition of the political environment relates to higher levels of electoral interest. However, we immediately encountered a puzzle. Taken together, the finding about the relationship between

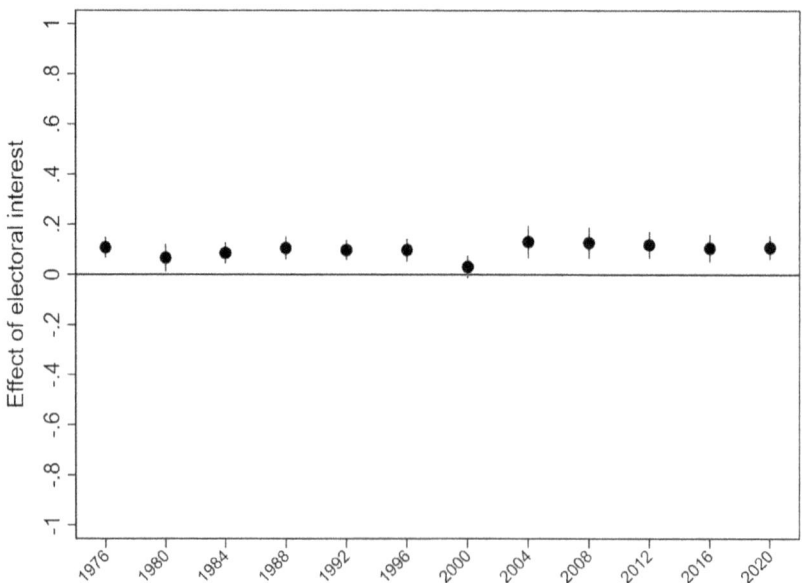

Figure 9 Effect of electoral interest on women's campaign participation: 1976–2020
Data from the ANES cumulative file and the 2020 ANES (weighted).

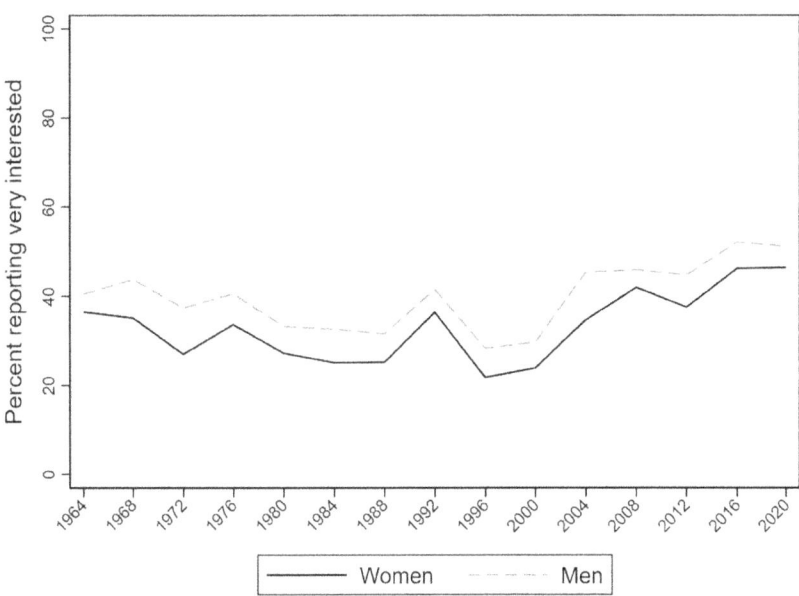

Figure 10 Percent of respondents reporting "very interested" in political campaigns by gender: 1976–2020

Data from the ANES cumulative file and the 2020 ANES (weighted).

Figure shows the percent of men and women who reported they were "very much interested" in political campaigns from 1976 to 2020. Electoral interest is a three-item measure, where respondents can say they are "Not much interested," "Somewhat interested," or "Very much interested" in the campaign so far in that year.

electoral interest and political activity and the findings in Section 1 about the closing of the gender gap in participation would lead us to expect a parallel narrowing of any gender gap in electoral interest. Instead, as shown in Figure 10, the gender gap in electoral interest has remained relatively constant for decades. Women's and men's levels of electoral interest, which have risen in the era of intense party polarization since the turn of the century, have moved in tandem. Women's political interest may have risen since the 1990s – but so has men's. The persistence of this disparity suggests that the convergence in participation does not result from any closing of the gender difference in electoral interest.

Figure 11 treats electoral interest as an intervening variable, operating between actual political events and the participation performed by individuals. What emerges is that gender congruence between respondents and the political environment *sometimes* produces a boost in women's electoral interest. The effect is positive in four of the twelve electoral cycles since 1976. As expected, we find significant effects on interest when the United States

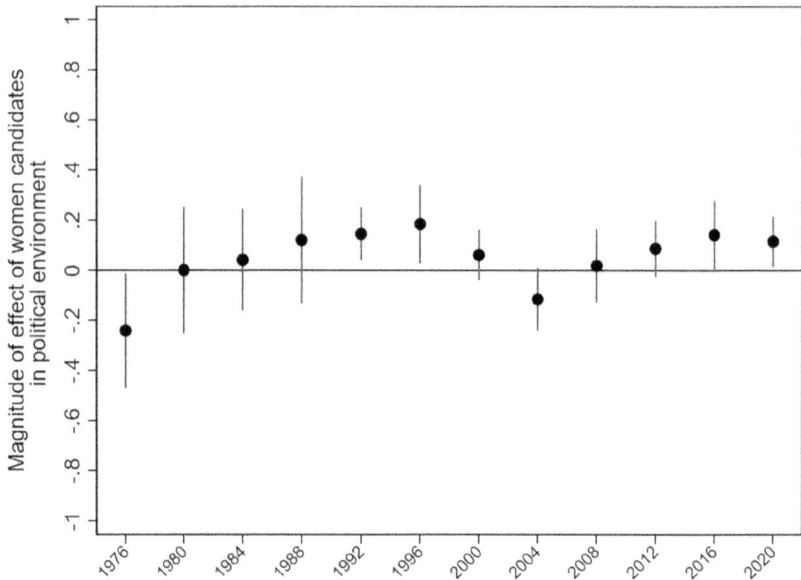

Figure 11 The effect of women politicians on women's electoral interest: 1976–2020

Data from the ANES cumulative file, the 2020 ANES (weighted), and the authors' CPE Database.

Respondents are coded as having visible women in their political environment if there is a female U.S. Senator or governor in their state or a female member of the U.S. House in their district who either won the election or was an incumbent in the year the ANES was conducted.

experienced the highly unusual "Year of the Woman" in 1992, when the numbers of women candidates tripled, and in the ensuing election in 1996. In addition, for reasons less readily apparent, we find effects that are barely significant in 2016 and 2020. We do not have an easy explanation as to why, at a time when gender issues figure importantly in *national* politics, having a visible woman in the *immediate political environment* of a respondent's state or congressional district should suddenly recur as significantly related to women's interest in elections.[30] Most importantly, the inclusion or exclusion of gender congruence in the political environment in the model has no meaningful effect on size, significance, or consistency of the relationship between electoral interest and political participation. Therefore, the indirect effect through political interest of gender correspondence in the political

---

[30] One avenue of exploration for future researchers is the suggestion from previous literature that collective, rather than dyadic, representation may have a greater effect on the participation, interest, and/or efficacy of female citizens (Atkeson and Carrillo 2007; Uhlaner and Scola 2015).

environment is not a major factor causing the significant narrowing of the gender gap in political participation.

3.6 Party, Race or Ethnicity, and Gender in the Political Environment: Does Congruence Increase Electoral Interest?

In our investigation of the indirect effect on participation through electoral interest of having visible women in the immediate political environment, we now return to a consideration of subgroups differentiated by gender and partisanship and, then, gender and race or ethnicity. Regarding partisan congruence, recall the logic we proposed earlier: a visible woman from the opposite party might serve to dampen electoral interest, not ignite it.[31] When we consider having party-congruent women in the political environment among all women, the results on interest look nearly identical to our results for all women in the political environment. The results are also not noticeably driven by either Republican or Democratic women, as we find no significant effect on electoral interest for any of the twelve presidential election cycles when we look separately at the two groups.

Figure 12 summarizes the findings when we consider the effect of candidate congruence on electoral interest across the six groups based on the intersection of gender and race or ethnicity. We find no effect of candidate congruence on the basis of gender and race or ethnicity on electoral interest for any of the groups except for Black women. Black women who have a visible Black woman – or, in fact, any woman regardless of race or ethnicity – in the immediate political environment show greater electoral interest.[32] Using other ANES items to test

---

[31] See, for example, Mariani et al. (2015).
[32] Kamala Harris, the only Black woman to serve as a senator or governor between 2008 and 2020, is the only Black woman senator or governor in our dataset. Since she represented the nation's most populous state in the Senate, we were concerned that our findings might be disproportionately affected by her high public visibility. Therefore, we performed an additional test, removing Kamala Harris and considering the effect of Black women in the political environment on Black women's interest for members of the House only. Per Appendix K, our results for Black women were the same whether we considered just members of the House or members of the House, Senate, and governors. We acknowledge that these findings could result from the fact that more generally, the districts where Black women run and win presumably have special characteristics. (See the findings in Palmer and Simon 2006 and 2012; as well as Thomsen and Swers 2017.) Still, using other ANES items that test for approval of congressional incumbents and candidates, we also found that Black female voters represented by Black women showed higher rates of such approval. Together with our findings on interest, these results may suggest some useful directions for future research. We also considered clustering at either the state or Congressional District level, or putting the data in a multilevel model. Given the ANES use of county data in their cluster sampling, clustering at the Congressional District is not feasible. We do not support clustering at the state level, since nearly all Black women candidates in our data are members of Congress, not senators or governors. We also do not find that this changes our results. Finally, given geographic segregation and our sample size of Black women, we would not have a sufficient sample in each cluster.

	Shared Race	Shared Gender	Shared Race and Gender	Shared Race – Woman Candidate
White Women	▓	.	.	.
White Men	▓	▓	▓	.
Black Women	.	+	+	+
Black Men	.	▓	.	.
Hispanic Women	.	.	.	.
Hispanic Men	.	▓	.	.

Figure 12 The effect of race-gender candidate and constituent congruence on electoral interest: Pooled 2008–2020 data

Data from the ANES cumulative file and the 2020 ANES (weighted), paired with candidate and incumbent data for every state and congressional district, collected by the authors (CPE Database). Shading signifies all respondents in this subgroup have at least one winner or incumbent with the same race or gender.

+ *positive association, significant at p<.05*
. *no effect*

for approval or disapproval of congressional incumbents and, separately, candidates, we also found that Black women voters represented by Black women officeholders or candidates showed higher rates of trust in government and also higher rates of approval of their congressional incumbents than Black women with representatives of other gender and race/ethnicity combinations.[33]

How are we to understand the finding that Black women are distinctive in having higher levels of electoral interest when the immediate political environment includes Black women – or, for that matter, women irrespective of race or ethnicity – in visible positions? We can specify several distinguishing

---

[33] One additional possibility is that, in contrast to our claim that representation causes electoral interest, Black women's electoral interest is responsible for increases in the number of Black women elected officials. However, this possibility would require that increases in Black women's electoral interest be accompanied by higher levels of participation and the election of more Black women. The absence of such findings makes this conjecture unlikely. Additionally, we looked at the association between Black women incumbents and Black women's electoral interest, as these incumbents were all elected before the ANES began asking about electoral interest. We find that the results remain robust to whether we look at both winning candidates and incumbents or just incumbents.

characteristics of Black women that are relevant to politics and to political participation more specifically. One is the direction of their political orientations. At least since 1972 (Gillespie and Brown 2019), they have been more strongly Democratic in their partisan leanings and vote choices than both Black men and, especially, white women, a political regularity that supports Junn and Matsuoka's (2020) contention that the oft-noted gender gap in presidential vote choice is also very much a race gap. At present, Black women are considered by Democratic Party elites and operatives to be the party's most faithful voters.

Beyond voting, Brown (2014) reports that Black women report relatively high levels of participation in such nontraditional activities as attending protests and signing petitions, a finding that also emerges from the ANES data (see Appendix O). Consistent with the findings of earlier work, Brown notes that, for Black women in particular, a sense of linked fate with other Black Americans significantly increases participation. Furthermore, detailed quantitative work finds that, compared to other groups, social capital and a desire to help the community matter more for Black women's political participation (Farris and Holman 2014; see also Shames 2017).

One possible explanation for the findings about race-gender congruence for Black women is Black women's growing political representation in Congress and state legislatures. Brown and Lemi (2020, p. 1620) speculate that Black women's electoral success may be a function of their "ability to engage and empathize with multiple communities of voters." Dowe (2020, p. 697) interprets Black women's political ambition as social rather than individual: "Black women have used political engagement to undermine that very marginalization, to sustain ambition, and to foster socialization that encourages independence and collective identity through families, organizations, and religious institutions" (see also Cole and Stewart 1996 and Gay and Tate 1998).

Such findings help to make sense of the result, specific to Black women, that seeing other visible Black or female representatives or candidates has a significant impact on interest. Still, we are left with puzzles. It is obvious neither why shared gender – that is, women of any race or ethnicity – but not shared race boosts electoral interest nor why electoral interest but not participation responds to the characteristics of the visible politicians in the immediate political environment. Furthermore, these effects on interest and approval do not appear to translate directly into a significant increase in Black women's turnout, activity in campaigns, or contributions. Nor do they explain Black men and women's greater political participation in the years when Obama was elected. Thus, while these findings are notable, they ultimately cannot explain the trends in political participation we observe.

3.7 Summary

In this section, we have explored from several perspectives the possibility that the key to changes in the gender gap for most kinds of political activity lies in politics itself, and we have come up short. We found that, in contrast to the upsurge in political activity by Black voters inspired by Barack Obama's presidential candidacy, Hillary Clinton's pathbreaking presidential campaign did not serve to mobilize women into politics. When we moved our gaze from proximate political factors to the longer-term change in the gender composition of those who contest and hold visible public office, we were no more successful in establishing that political context is responsible for diminishing the gender gap in political activity. We found no direct impact on women's political activity of the presence of a visible woman candidate or incumbent in the immediate political environment of the congressional district or state.

We replicated the finding that, during the 1990s, the presence of a visible woman politician in the immediate political environment had a positive impact on electoral interest. That effect faded with the turn of the century only to reappear, though less strongly, in 2016 and 2020. In undertaking the analysis of the possible indirect effect of the gender composition of the political environment on political activity through its impact on electoral interest, we uncovered another confusing finding. Although electoral interest is a significant predictor of political participation, and although the disparity between men and women in participation has narrowed over the last half-century, the gender gap in electoral interest is unchanged. Both women and men are more interested in electoral politics than they were in 1976 or in 1996, but men have consistently been somewhat more interested than women.

Drilling down, we considered the intersectional groups defined by gender and party and by gender and race or ethnicity. We constructed a new data set that incorporates information – including the gender and race or ethnicity of the major-party incumbents and candidates – for every election for House, Senate, and governor in the presidential election years between 2008 and 2020. Whether we considered the direct effect on political activity or an indirect effect through electoral interest from correspondence on the basis of gender and partisanship or gender and race/ethnicity, we found – with one important exception – nothing significant. Although the sample sizes are limited, we take seriously the critical exception to the pattern of null findings: Black women are more interested in elections when there is a visible woman, or a Black woman, in their political environment.

The bottom line is that changes to the political environment do not provide an explanation for changes in the gender gap in political activity. To understand gender differences in participation, we must look elsewhere.

4 Is It Social-Structural Resources?

4.1 Structural Resources and Political Participation

The various aspects of the political context just considered in Section 3 seem not to be very helpful in understanding changes in the gender gap in participation. So what does explain the change? Students of political participation in the United States agree that any explanation of individual differences in political activity must consider a variety of long- and short-term individual and contextual factors. Among the factors most consistently associated with political activity, however, are a set of concrete resources – most importantly, education, income, and the civic skills exercised in nonpolitical domains of adult life such as work, church, and nonpolitical organizations (Verba, Schlozman, and Brady 1995; Burns, Schlozman, and Verba 2001; see also Tate 1991 and Calhoun-Brown 1996). In this section, we focus on long-term social structural factors associated with class and consider whether changes in relative gender differences in education or income are helpful in explaining the diminution of participatory disparities between women and men. Because the distribution of resources in the United States varies substantially by race and ethnicity, to the extent our data allow, we take, as usual, an intersectional perspective.

The class-based resources of income and education have a dual role in our analysis. Not only are they significant resources for political action, but they are themselves bases of political contestation. From school libraries and student loans to taxes and Medicaid eligibility, issues involving education or income are rarely absent from American politics. A corollary to this observation is that many issues engage conflict between forces anchored in social class. Such a circumstance implies the potential compromise of the principle of equal protection of interests. As we mentioned in Section 1, when participatory inequalities are linked to differences in preferences and needs for government policy, then political equality may be jeopardized. Income groups have long been relevant for politics; over the past decade, educational stratification has become increasingly associated with partisan vote choices. Participatory disparities on the basis of income and education imply inequalities of political voice and, thus, a selective set of messages to policymakers (Carnes 2013).

4.2 Changing Resource Levels

Educational attainment, a critical resource for political activity, has risen steadily over the past century. More relevant to our concerns, the long-term secular trend of men receiving more college degrees than women reversed sometime in the 1980s. Figure 13 shows, for the eight decades between 1940 and 2020, the proportion with a college degree for men and women ages 25–29 (on the left) and adults 25 and older (on the right). By the 1990s women in their late twenties were more likely than men to have graduated from college. By the 2010 Census, women had overtaken men in the share of college graduates among adults 25 and over.

Figure 14 presents the data by gender and race or ethnicity. Several patterns emerge. For each of the groups, the proportion of adults 25 and over who have attained a bachelor's degree has risen over time. Notably, for both men and women, college attainment is higher for white adults than for Black or, especially, Hispanic adults, a pattern with implications for equal political voice. In each group, at some point, women overtook men in the proportion with a bachelor's degree – a pattern that emerged first for Black, then for Hispanic, and, later, for white adults 25 and over.[34] The causes of these gender gaps may be shared across racial groups or may be unique to a particular group;

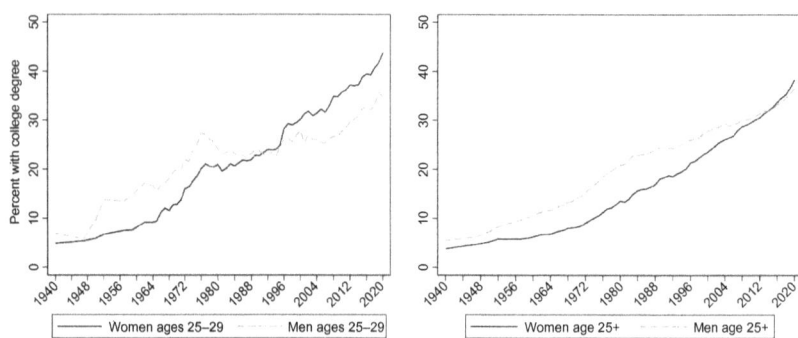

Figure 13 Percent of young adults (ages 25–29) and all adults (ages 25+) with a college degree by gender: 1940–2020

Data from the U.S. Census Bureau Current Population Survey. In 1990, the Census changed the method used to assess whether respondents had completed a bachelor's degree or higher. Until 1990, respondents were asked, first, the number of years of school attended and then whether they had completed the final year of schooling. Starting in 1990, respondents answered a single question about the highest degree completed.

---

[34] For an alternative perspective on women's relative educational gains that emphasizes how young men on the lower rungs of the economic ladder – especially young Black and Hispanic men – are being left behind, see Reeves (2022).

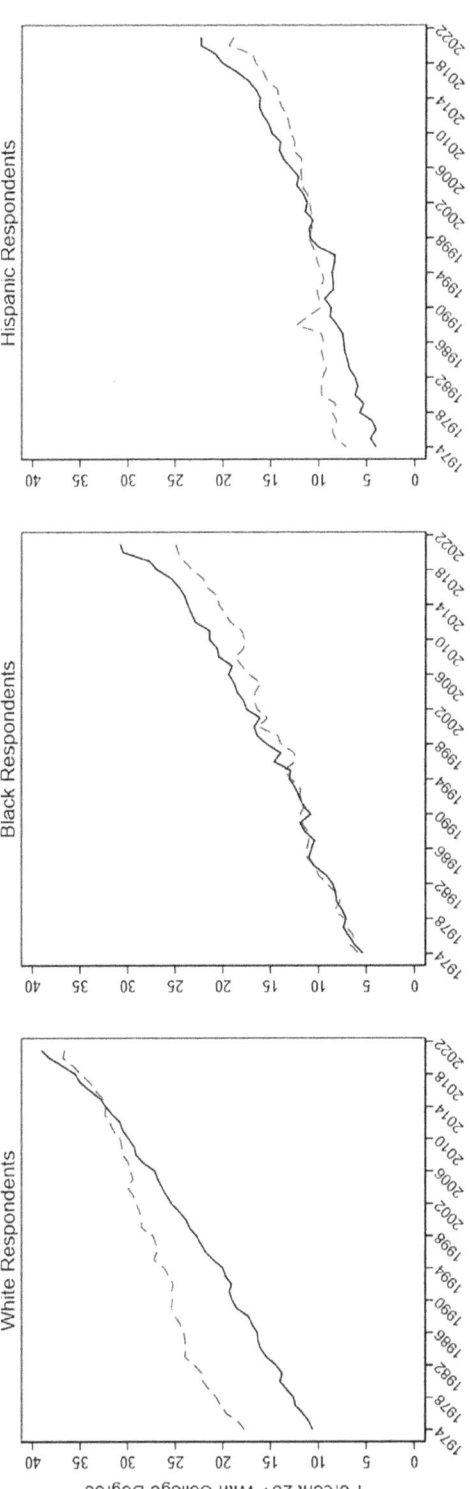

Figure 14 Percent of white, Black, and Hispanic adults, 25 and older, with a college degree by gender: 1974–2020

Data from the U.S. Census Bureau Current Population Survey. In 1990, the Census changed the method used to assess whether respondents had completed a bachelor's degree or higher. Until 1990, respondents were asked, first, the number of years of school attended and then whether they had completed the final year of schooling. Starting in 1990, respondents answered a single question about the highest degree completed.

considerable attention has been paid, for example, to the magnitude of the gender gap in Black educational attainment and to its direct and indirect roots in a variety of factors – among them, mass incarceration, relative access to individual and household resources, and experiences in school.[35]

While strongly correlated and both associated with participation, income and education are not the same, however. Women's long-standing disadvantage with respect to such economic resources as income, wealth, and job status is well known – as are the strides women have made in the last half-century.[36] Although there has been some convergence in the period since 1960, women's incomes continue, on average, to lag men's. The story behind long-standing gender inequalities in income, one best left to economists, involves the complex interaction of several processes including rates of work-force participation for men and women, the relative earnings of women and men in the work force, and changing family patterns.

As shown in Figure 15, women's labor force participation rose steadily until the 1990s when it leveled off. At the same time, men's labor force participation has decreased, although at a slower rate. As shown in Figure 16, these patterns obtain within the three groups defined by race or ethnicity. The gender gap in labor force participation is especially wide for Hispanic, and narrow for Black workers, a result driven by larger differences among the three groups in men's labor force participation. Having a job is in many ways enabling of political participation.[37] Those with jobs have opportunities to develop work-based civic skills, and the workplace is a common site for requests to take part in politics. And, of course, jobs pay wages – the most important source of income for the overwhelming share of American adults.

Similarly, the long-term gap in earnings between women and men – measured in Figure 17 in terms of "usual weekly earnings" – has declined but has not closed.[38] In fact, while the 2020 gender difference in weekly earnings was roughly half of what it was in 1979, much of the progress took place in the

---

[35] See, e.g., Hauser (1993); Massey et al. (2006); McDaniel et al. (2011); DiPrete and Buchmann (2013); and Autor et al. (2019).

[36] Cleveland, Stockdale, and Murphy (2000); Williams (2001); Blau, Brinton, and Grusky (2006); Blau and Kahn (2007 and 2017); Chang (2010); Bryner and Weber (2013); Blackburn, Jarman, and Racko (2016); and Killewald, Pfeffer, and Schachner (2017). On the interaction of race or ethnicity with gender, see Conley (2010) and Grumbach, Sahn, and Staszak (2020).

[37] However, in their investigation of the consequence of women's ambivalence toward going to work full time, Burns and Jardina (2016) demonstrate that it is too simple to assume that increased workforce participation inevitably leads to greater political activity.

[38] According to the U.S. Bureau of Labor Statistics (2024): "Usual weekly earnings ... represent earnings before taxes and other deductions and include any overtime pay, commissions, or tips usually received (at the main job in the case of multiple jobholders). Prior to 1994, respondents were asked how much they usually earned per week. Since January 1994, respondents have been asked to identify the easiest way for them to report earnings (hourly, weekly, biweekly, twice

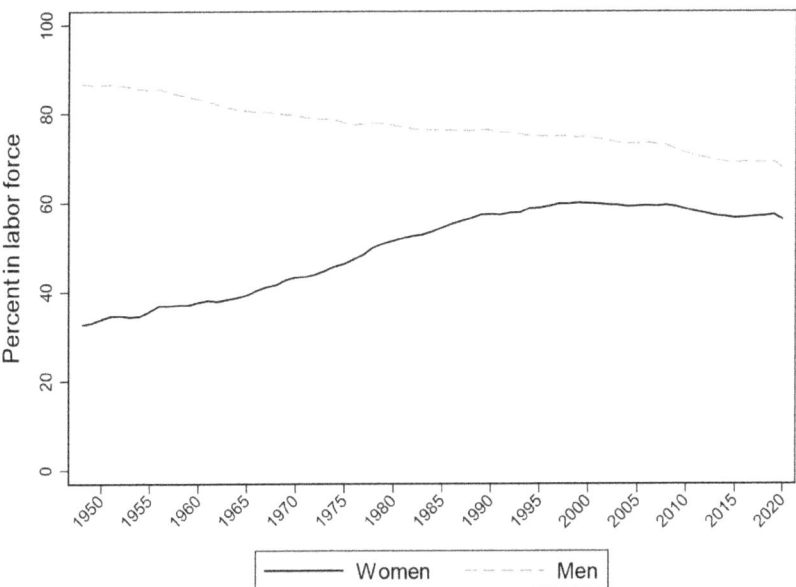

Figure 15 Labor force participation by gender: 1948–2020
Data from the U.S. Department of Labor. Figure shows the percentage of men and women in the civilian noninstitutional population, sixteen years of age and older that are employed or actively looking for work.

1980s. Between 2004 and 2020, the disparity was basically static, varying between 80 and 82 percent.[39] There are a variety of reasons that women's earnings trail men's, including that women are more likely than men to work part- rather than full-time and that, among full-time workers, women, on average, put in fewer hours on the job than men do. Occupational segregation also means that occupations with a greater number of women are also often paid less than occupations with a greater number of men (Murphy and Oesch 2016). Data presented in Figure 18 show that this same pattern obtains within groups defined by race or ethnicity. While there are group differences in earnings, with white workers consistently earning more than Black or Hispanic workers, the gender gap in earnings between Black women and Black men and between Hispanic women and men is narrower than that between white women and men.

The picture is somewhat more complicated when we consider household income – which includes income from all sources, not just earnings – in Figure 19. Because the number of wage earners in a household is among the

monthly, monthly, annually, or other) and how much they usually earn in the reported time period."
[39] U.S. Bureau of Labor Statistics (2021).

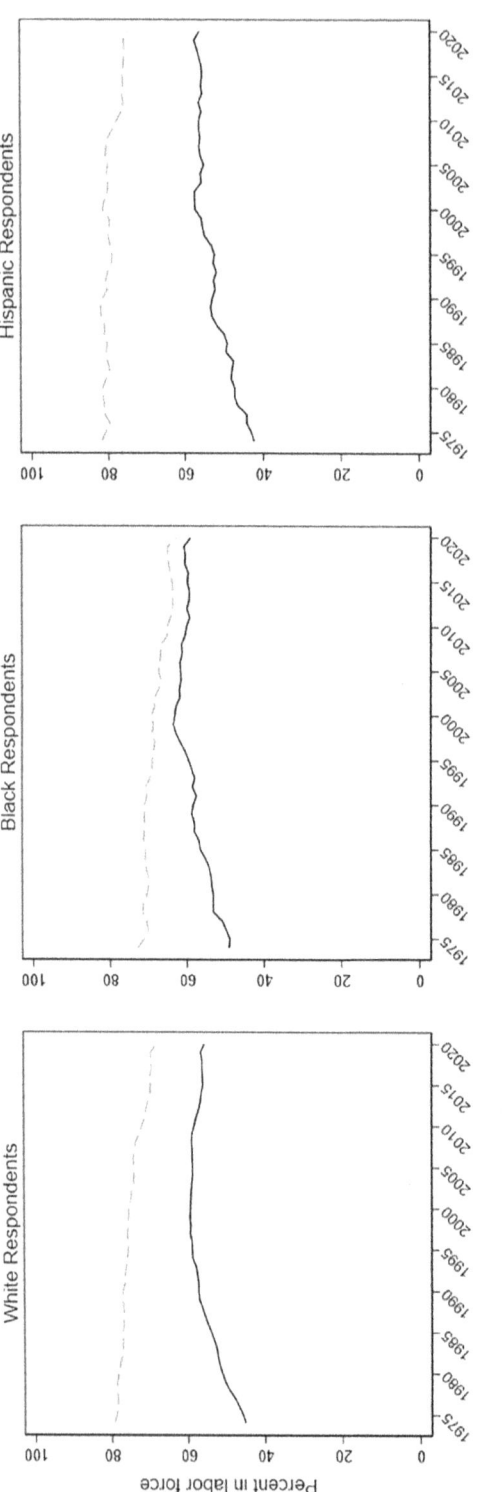

Figure 16 Labor force participation of white, Black, and Hispanic Americans by gender: 1974–2020

Data from the U.S. Department of Labor. Figure shows the percentage of men and women in the civilian noninstitutional population, sixteen years of age and older that are employed or actively looking for work.

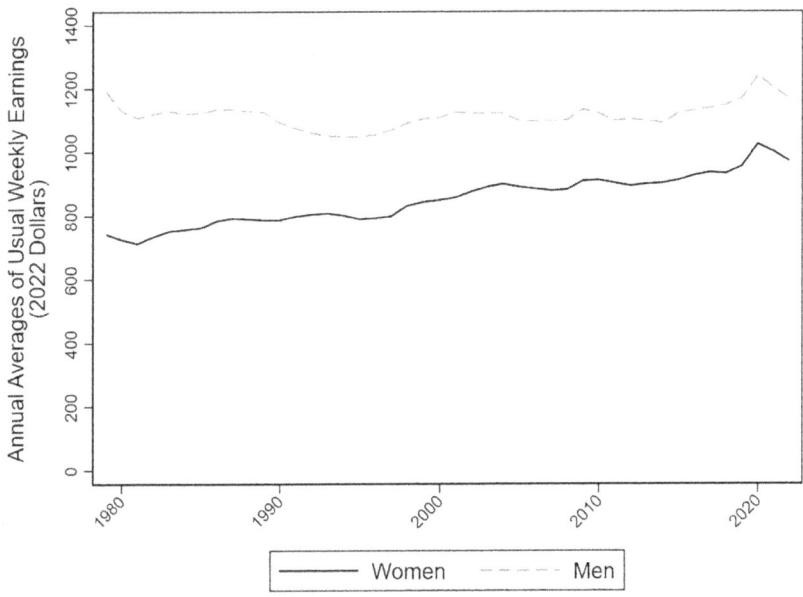

Figure 17 Annual averages of "usual weekly earnings" among full-time wage and salary workers by gender over time (2022 dollars): 1979–2022
Data from the Bureau of Labor Statistics (BLS). "Usual Weekly Earnings" is a BLS term.

most important predictors of household income, household income reflects family structure. Within the whole population, as well as within each of the three groups defined by race or ethnicity (Figure 20), married couple households have consistently had the highest median household income followed by households headed by men with no spouse present and last, some distance behind, households headed by women with no spouse present. While we have seen considerable convergence when it comes to the gender wage gap, there has been no parallel diminution of the disparity in median household income between female-headed and male-headed households. When we consider that 80 percent of single-parent households are run by women and that four in ten children are being raised by "breadwinner moms," the significance of the income deficit of female-headed households becomes apparent (Houston 2013; Pew 2013).[40]

---

[40] Racial and ethnic groups differ with respect to family structure. U.S. Census data (2020) show Black families are much more likely to be headed by single women. See also Pew (2013) and Glynn (2019) on single moms, and Bernhard, Shames, and Teele (2021) for a study on breadwinning, motherhood, and running for office.

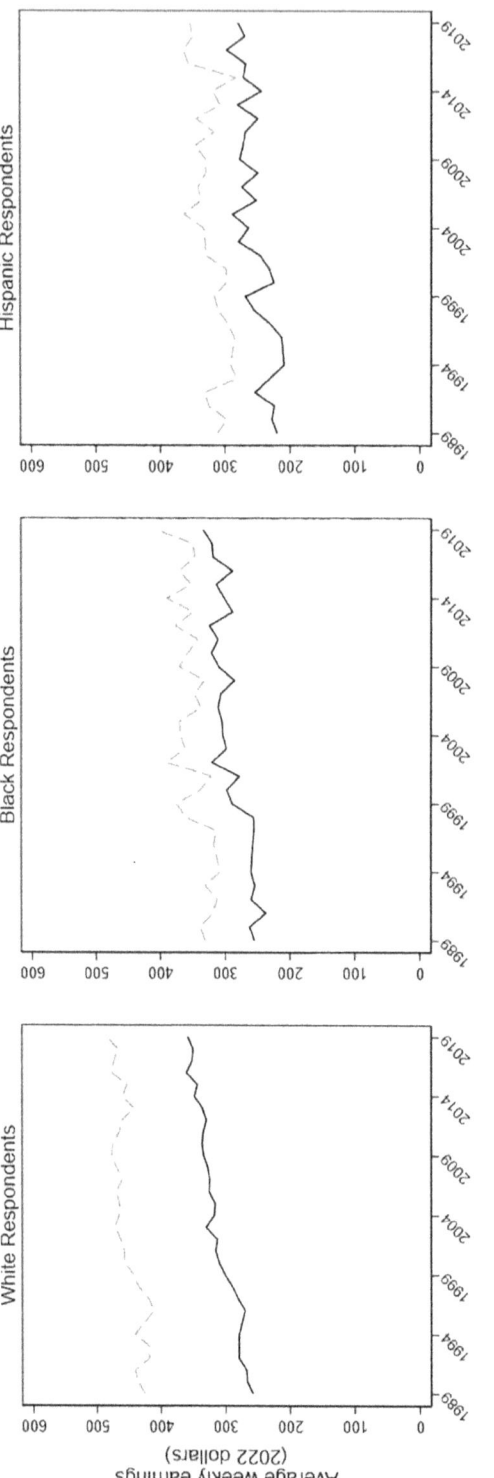

Figure 18 Annual averages of "usual weekly earnings" of white, Black, and Hispanic Americans by gender over time (2022 dollars): 1989–2020
Data from the BLS. "Usual Weekly Earnings" is a BLS term.

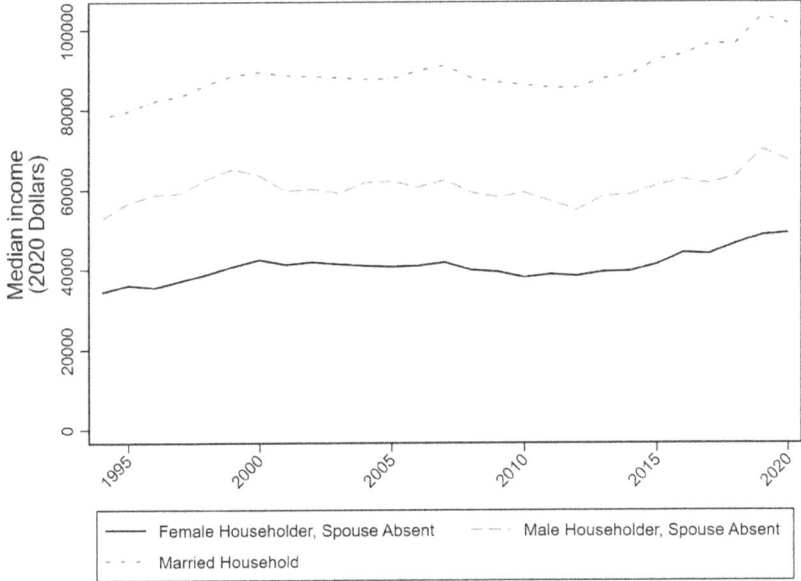

Figure 19 Median household income by gender and marital status (2020 dollars): 1994–2020
Data from the U.S. Census Bureau Current Population Survey. "Married Household" refers to families with two heads of household, while "Female Householder" and "Male Householder" refer to families with a female or male head of household.

4.3 Structural Resources and the Gender Gap in Participation: Effects over Time

To assess the consequences over time of structural resources like education and income for the gender gap in political participation, we return to our concern with *levels* and *effects* (see Section 2.3). At any particular time, the gender gap in activity reflects either gender differences in the amount of various participatory factors or gender differences in the extent to which such factors have an impact on political activity, or both. In turn, variations over time in the size of the gender gap in participation reflect relative changes in how much of various participatory factors men and women have at their command or changes, for women or men, in the impact on participation of these factors, or both. We have just seen that the last half-century has witnessed significant changes in the disparity between women and men in their relative stockpiles of the class-based resources of education and income. We now turn to an analysis of how such variations in levels of these participatory factors work together with any

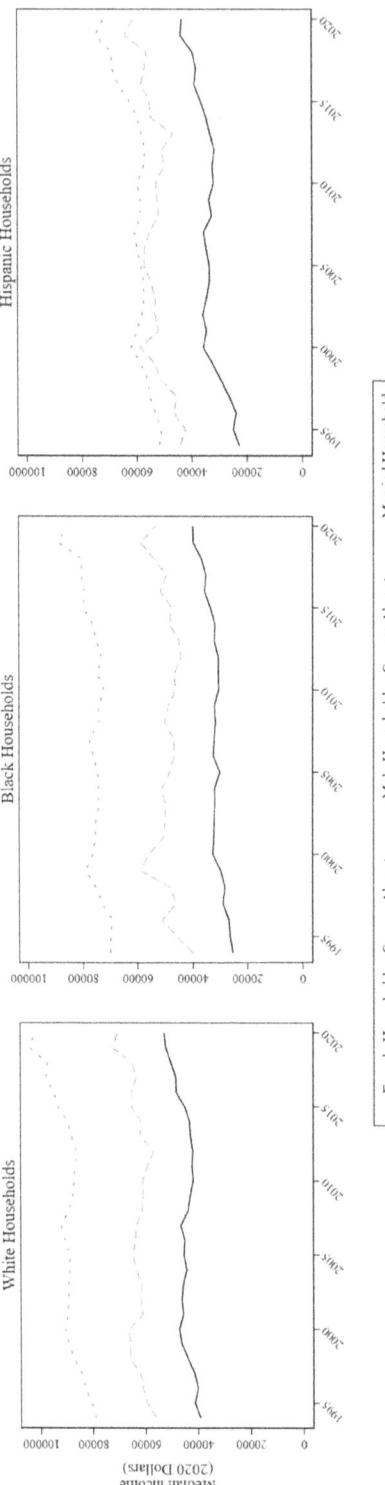

Figure 20 Median income of white, Black, and Hispanic households by gender and marital status over time (2020 dollars): 1994–2020

Data from the U.S. Census Bureau Current Population Survey. "Married Household" refers to families with two heads of household, while "Female Householder" and "Male Householder" refer to families with one female or male head of household.

changes over time in their relative effects on participation to influence the gender gap in participation.

We begin by considering the *effect* of both education and income on men and women's participation over time. To do this, we use statistical models that assess the association between education and income, and three forms of participation in ANES data – voting, campaign participation, and donating money to candidates or parties. We estimate these models in repeated cross-sections of respondents from 1976 through 2020, conducting separate regressions for each four-year period. We undertake our analyses separately for men and women, as well as for the six intersectional subgroups. The objective is to ascertain whether, for any group, changes in the impact of education or income on participation might be responsible for changes in the gender gap regarding a particular activity. That is, if the association between education or income and a particular political act becomes relatively stronger for women than for men, the gender gap in participation would narrow. Conversely, if the association between education or income and a particular political act becomes relatively weaker for women than for men, the gender gap in participation would widen.

In statistical terms, changes in effect would be signaled by a significant change from year to year in the size of the coefficient on education or income for any form of participation. For such changes in the effects of either education or income to narrow the gender gap in political activity, the coefficients on either of these factors would either increase significantly more for women than for men, decrease significantly more for men than for women, or both. In all models, we control for education, household income, political interest, and other factors impacting political participation, including employment status, marital status, age, and church attendance.

In Figure 21, we use data from 1976 to 2020 to show the effect of education and income on voting, the form of political participation in which, by far, the largest share of American adults engages. The patterns are quite clear. For both women and men, income and, especially, education have a positive impact on turnout. These effects are relatively stable over time and are substantively similar for men and women Although it may have diminished somewhat in recent elections, the impact of education on voting is somewhat stronger than that of income, which is consistently positive but not always significant.

Data about the impact of education and income on campaign activity and making campaign donations for the same period (which can be found in Appendix D) show similar patterns. The effects are stronger for education than for income, stable over time, and not significantly different for women and men. That educational attainment consistently has a stronger participatory effect than income for political donations is perhaps anomalous. Prior research (see, for

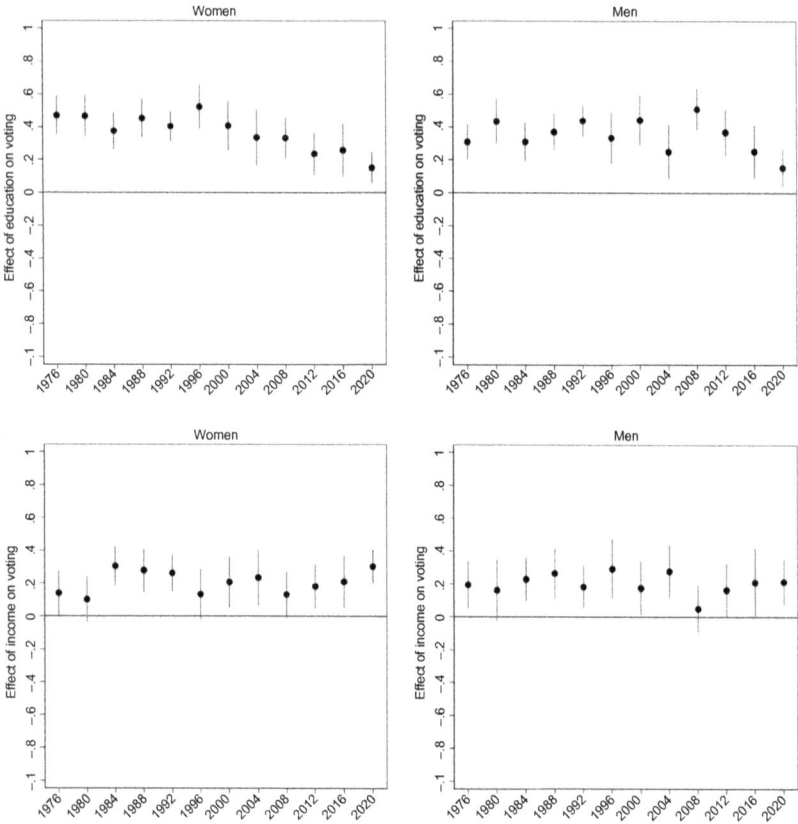

Figure 21 The effects of education and income on voting by gender: 1976–2020
Data from the ANES cumulative file and the 2020 ANES (weighted).

See Appendix D for regression results and other tests of significance by year and on other dependent variables, and Appendix E for further results by race-gender subgroups.

example, Schlozman, Brady, and Verba 2018, chap. 3) has shown income, not education, to be more strongly associated with making political contributions.

When we repeat this analysis for the six intersectional groups defined by gender and race or ethnicity, the same overall patterns obtain. Because ANES sample sizes for Black and Hispanic respondents were small until recently, we undertook this analysis for 2008–2020 only. Presumably, the more limited number of cases is responsible for the fact that, even though the overall patterns are evident, there is less stability in the coefficients from year to year and, while correct in direction, relatively few of the relationships are statistically significant.[41]

---

[41] Full data analyses across all six groups are in Appendix E.

4.4 Structural Resources and the Gender Gap in Participation: The Consequences of Changing Levels of Education and Income

These findings about effects suggest that we should expect the changes over time we reviewed earlier in the section in the levels of participatory factors commanded by men and women – namely, the disappearance of women's educational deficit and the diminution of the gender disparity in income – to have consequences for the gender gap in participation. We are now in a position to assess how changing relative levels of education and income work together with relatively unchanging, but significant, effects on participation to influence the magnitude of the gender gap in political activity. To do so, we pose a counterfactual: What would the gender gap in participation look like today if, after 1976, women had not made gains relative to men in both income and, especially, education? Once again, we use the over-time data from the ANES and multiple regression analysis. For each year from 1976 to 2020, we use regression analyses to generate predicted levels of political participation for men and for women based on key ingredients of participation, including levels of education and income, among the other variables, discussed in Section 2, found to matter for participation.

Figure 22 shows the results of these complicated analyses for the gender gap in voting for the presidential election years between 1976 and 2020. Each figure shows the observed (or actual) size of the gender gap in turnout with the solid line, as well as the predicted size of the gender gap in turnout had educational attainment (on the left) or income (on the right) been stuck at its level in 1976, but all other factors – for example, employment status or age – had varied over time, shown by the dashed line. Note that the dashed line for predicted turnout remains below or near 0 in the graphs for both education and income. Had levels of educational attainment and income not increased for both men and women – but, especially, for women – since 1976, we would have predicted a consistent, though slightly diminishing, gender disparity across the entire period with men more likely than women to vote. However, the data for the observed gender turnout gap show that, over time, men's turnout advantage did not persist. It disappeared – shown by the solid line for observed turnout crossing 0 in 2004. After that, the turnout gap reversed, with women voting at higher rates. That the two lines diverge in both panels of the figure suggests that increases in educational attainment, on the left, and income, on the right, are associated with higher turnout.[42]

---

[42] The slight variations over time in the magnitude of the gender gap in voting when education is held at 1976 levels reflect changes in other variables associated with turnout, possibly correlated with education or income. While we hold constant those variables, we cannot hold constant their ability to shape other factors.

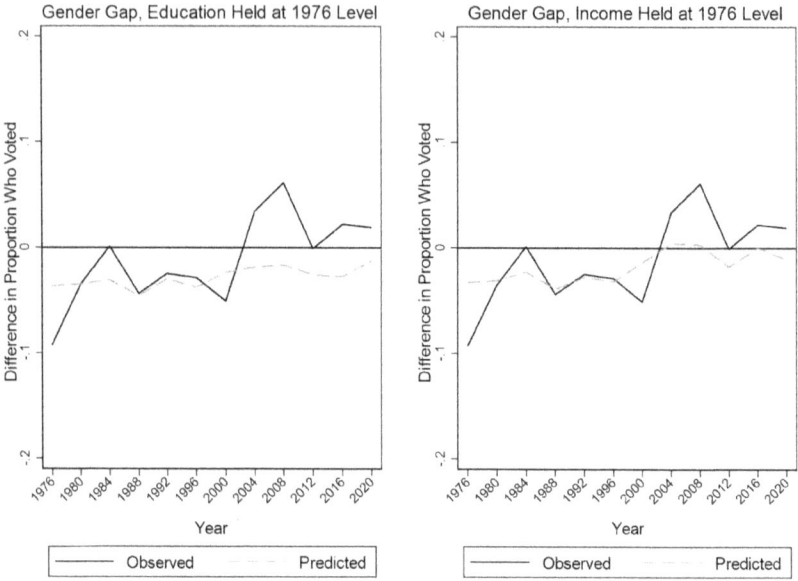

Figure 22 Comparison of observed and predicted voting by gender holding education at 1976 levels: 1976–2020

Data from the ANES cumulative file and the 2020 ANES (weighted). This figure plots the predicted gap between women and men in voting from 1976 to 2020 when education (left panel) or income (right panel) are held at 1976 levels for all respondents, compared to the observed gap in the same period.

1 above the horizontal line at 0 represents a 10 percentage point advantage for women, while −.1, below the 0-line, represents a 10-point advantage for men.

These analyses are, of course, based on a counterfactual. Disparities between women and men in education and income have not been stuck since 1976. Instead, gender differences in educational attainment have disappeared and gender inequalities in incomes have been reduced, which leads to the conclusion that women's gains in income and, especially, education, relative to men's, have been critical in closing and, eventually, reversing the gender gap in voter turnout.

In the name of saving space – and not taxing readers' patience – we do not present parallel analyses for campaign participation and campaign contributions, which are presented in Appendix M. The overall patterns reflect what we have just seen. If either income or, especially, education had been fixed at its 1976 level, we would expect little change in the participatory gender gap. Instead, women made gains relative to men in both income and, especially, education with the result that, as we saw in Section 1, the gender gap in campaign activity closed and the gender gap in making campaign donations narrowed but did not disappear.

The next step is to replicate this analysis intersectionally. We expect that women's gains relative to men, especially with respect to education, play a role in shaping the participatory gender gap within each of the groups defined by race or ethnicity. Recall from Figure 14, that in each group, at some point, women overtook men in the proportion with a bachelor's degree – first among Black Americans, then among Hispanic Americans, and finally among white Americans. But as we proceed, we keep in mind that prior work finds that resources, like education, do not predict participation for Black and Hispanic women as well as they do for white women (Laurison, Brown, and Rastogi 2022).[43]

Because we are interested in how changing levels of education and income shape political participation across race and ethnicity, we sought to find a starting year for our analyses that would produce sufficiently large samples to make comparisons over time. The analyses that take into account levels of education and income for groups defined by race and ethnicity begin in 1992.[44] The smaller numbers of cases of Black and Hispanic women and men affect our ability to make claims about predicted levels of participation. However, as shown in Figure 23, the general pattern for men and women as large groups also obtains for the six intersectional groups: the associations were always in the right direction though often not statistically significant. Taken together, these findings suggest that relative gains by women with respect to education and income in all three groups defined by race or ethnicity would contribute to narrowing the gender gap in participation.

---

[43] One theory for why Black Americans participate in politics at rates greater than their relative socioeconomic status is that a sense of racial group consciousness or linked fate (Dawson 1994) acts as a psychological force motivating Black political engagement (see also Chong and Rogers 2005). We ran regression models predicting the three forms of participation controlling for racial consciousness and find that it does not affect the relationship between our other main independent variables of interest and participation. We also note Philpot and Walton (2014) are reasonably critical of earlier work on racial consciousness, which they suggest overlooks the very real barriers to engagement that defined the economic and policy oppression of the Deep South under Jim Crow, some of which persisted even after the Voting Rights Act.

[44] 1992 is the first year that the ANES has close to 100 respondents in each of the following groups: Black men and women and Hispanic men and women. 1992 also has the largest subsamples of these groups until the ANES introduced oversamples in 2008. Because we need one starting year, which we can use to estimate the predicted levels of education and income, we selected 1992 as our starting year for these analyses. Most other analyses start in 2008, with the oversampling of Black and Latino respondents, as the 2008–2020 surveys *consistently* have samples of over 200 Black women, Black men, Hispanic women, and Hispanic men. Again, these are still smaller samples, but they are the best we can do with ANES data, which has the benefit of asking these questions consistently over time – making possible our "levels" analyses.

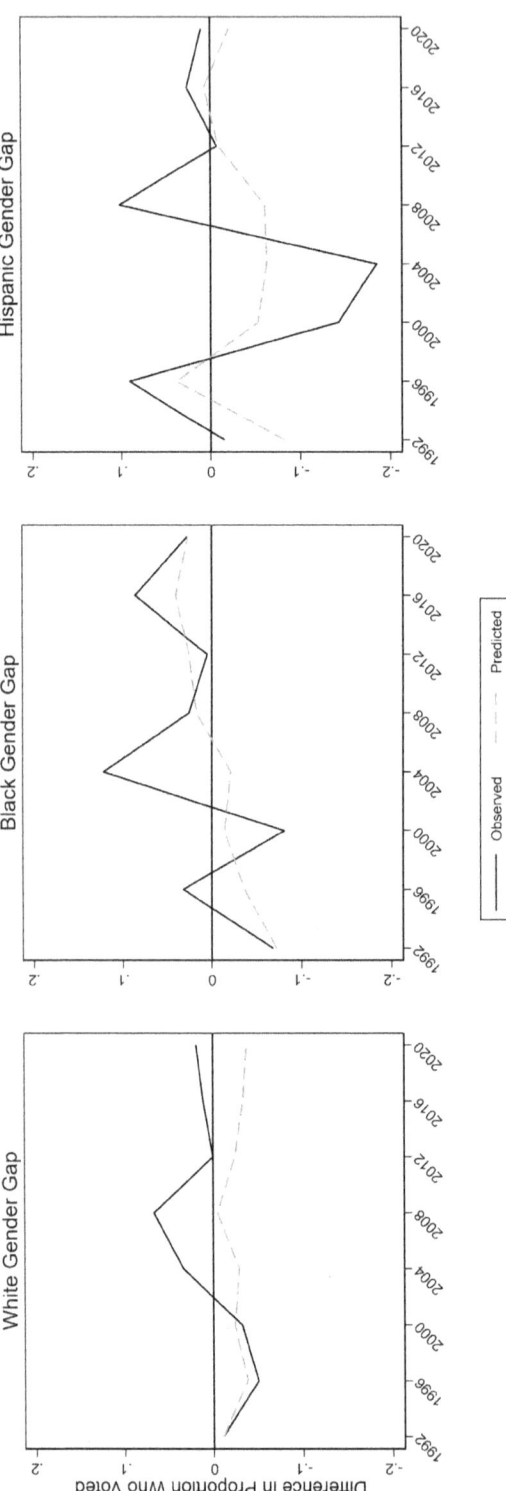

Figure 23 Comparison of observed and predicted voting by gender and race or ethnicity over time holding education at 1992 levels: 1992–2020

Data from the ANES cumulative file and the 2020 ANES (weighted). This figure plots, separately for white, Black, and Hispanic respondents, the predicted gap in voting between men and women from 1992 to 2020 when education is held at its 1992 levels, compared to the observed gap in the same period. .1 above the horizontal line at 0 represents a 10 percentage point advantage for women, while −.1, below the 0-line, represents a 10-point advantage for men.

The three panels of Figure 23 present the results for voter turnout, comparing observed levels of voting with predicted levels of voting when education is held at its 1992 levels, separately for white, Black, and Hispanic respondents. Not surprisingly, the data for white respondents track what we saw when we considered the period 1992–2020 for the whole population. The results are less stable for Black and Hispanic respondents, the consequence, we suspect, of small sample sizes. Still, we can note that – contrary to the predicted disparity based on 1992 levels of education for each group – the gender gap in turnout reverses for all three groups, evidence that relative educational gains by women in each group are an important part of the story of the closing and reversal of the gaps in voter turnout. We find more variable results for the relationship between predicted income and voter turnout, likely reflecting the weaker relationship between these two factors and the consistent strength of education in explaining who votes and participates (see Appendix N).[45]

4.5 Summary

Having failed to locate the roots of the diminution of the gender gap in political participation in the world of politics, in this section we investigated the consequences of important social-structural changes. Over the last forty years, women have been more likely than men to graduate from college, and women are now, in the aggregate, better educated than men. In addition, although far from disappearing, men's long-standing advantage with respect to income has narrowed over the last half-century.

Previous research has demonstrated that socioeconomic status provides important resources for political activity. Our data confirm that education and income are associated with political participation for both women and men and that there is no significant gender difference in the participatory effects of these resources. We used simulations to demonstrate that, had levels of education and income remained unchanged since 1976, the gender gap in political participation would still be with us. In sum, the convergence in rates of political activity reflects, at least in part, social-structural changes with implications far beyond the arena of citizen politics.

5 The Dollar Gap

So far, we have shown a pattern of the closing of the gender gap in key forms of political activity in the twenty-first century and argued that the process is related to women's gains with respect to the critical participatory resources of income

---

[45] In keeping with past work on Black and Hispanic participation (Shingles (1981); Mangum (2003); Stokes (2003); Sanchez (2006); Philpot and Walton (2007); and Masuoka (2008), we considered whether including linked fate in our models affected key findings about candidate racial/ethnic congruence or structural resources. Appendix G shows it did not.

and, especially, education. In this section, we discuss an important exception to this pattern: political contributions. Gender disparities in political giving have either held steady or, if viewed from a different perspective, widened over the last half-century.

5.1 Introductory Matters: Donating as a Special Form of Participation

Making financial donations to political campaigns and causes differs in important ways from the other forms of political activity we have been discussing. With respect to casting a ballot, the principle of one person, one vote equalizes the input of those who vote in any particular election. When it comes to getting involved in electoral campaigns, there are no such limits beyond the constraints imposed by our finite quantities of spare time. Still, even the most leisured person has only 24 hours in a day, which limits the extent to which the most active campaigner can out-campaign the least active campaigner. Such a ceiling does not exist when it comes to political contributions. The wealthiest are not only more likely to make a political contribution but in a position to donate at levels unimaginable to all but a few Americans. The married couple who together were the top donors in the 2020 election cycle gave more than $218 million, a sum that is many, many times what most people earn in a lifetime (OpenSecrets 2023a). In short, when dollars, rather than votes or hours, are the metric of political input, political inequalities are multiplied.

The story told in this section is a uniquely American one. Compared to other affluent democracies, campaign finance arrangements in the United States rely very little on public sources of support – for example, subsidies to political candidates and parties or provision for free media time – and permit much greater latitude to individuals to contribute whatever sums their bank accounts allow (e.g., Scarrow 2007 and, for a review of the literature on gender and political donations, see Norris and van Es 2016 and Tolley, Besco, and Sevi 2022). Shames (2017, Table 3.2) notes that among OECD countries, the United States underperforms substantially in public funding for candidates, parties, free or subsidized media access, and limits on campaign spending.

Over the period we have been examining, the campaign finance environment has changed in many ways ranging from the laws and regulations governing political contributions to the technologies for raising money and communicating with potential donors. Building upon the decision in *Buckley* v. *Valeo* (1976), a series of federal court decisions have defined making political contributions as a form of speech under the First Amendment.[46] The institutional consequence has

---

[46] For discussion of the recent judicial decisions that have created the current environment for campaign giving and the extent to which total campaign giving at the federal level is dominated

been the emergence of a variety of vehicles for collecting political money in unlimited amounts, not all of which are required to disclose their donors. More generally, the lid has more or less been lifted off the limits on what individuals can donate, and aggregate campaign spending has soared. According to data from the Campaign Finance Institute, between 1974 and 2018, in constant dollars, the average cost of a major-party candidacy for the U.S. House rose 6.24 times, and the average cost of a major-party candidacy for the U.S. Senate rose 5.76 times.[47] As summarized in a report on the changes to the campaign finance regime: "individuals with means can associate more freely and efficiently in collective efforts to influence the political process. Moreover, they may now do so with greater opportunity to arrange their participation with limited or no public disclosure" (Persily, Bauer, and Ginsberg 2018, p. 10). Welcome to the American campaign finance arms race.

With the fall of legal constraints and the rise in campaign costs, making political contributions has assumed greater importance in the portfolio of individual participatory acts. Like all activists, contributors donate for a variety of reasons. A survey of candidate donors in 2016 asked respondents – a group that skewed somewhat male, substantially older, and overwhelmingly white – about a half dozen possible motivations for making campaign contributions including, for example, acting out of a sense of civic duty or seeking to be part of a social network. The most common – which 66 percent of respondents rated as very or extremely important – was seeking to influence policy. When asked about a recent contribution in a particular race for the U.S. House, 44 percent of donors replied that it was very or extremely important that they would have access on a policy issue and 37 percent that they would get a phone call returned. Among max-out House donors, the responses were 49 percent and 47 percent, respectively.[48]

These figures suggest that our current regime of free-for-all campaign finance raises questions about political equality and that we need to pay attention to the extent to which not only campaign donors, but, perhaps more importantly, the entire pool of campaign dollars is unrepresentative of the American public in terms of policy preferences and other politically relevant characteristics.

---

by a handful of very generous donors, see Schlozman, Brady, and Verba (2018, pp. 212–214 and 244–250).

[47] Calculated from data given by the Campaign Finance Institute website (2023). There is strong evidence that, in a contested federal election, the big spender usually wins. Between 2000 and 2020, in a majority of the election years, the top spender won more than 90 percent of House elections and more than 80 percent of Senate elections (OpenSecrets 2023a). Box-Steffensmeier (1996) finds that incumbents often amass large "war chests" which stave off high-quality challengers. And there seems to be consensus that campaign spending is productive for challengers who do enter the race (Gerber 2004 and Jacobson 2006).

[48] Figures from Hersh and Schaffner (2017), who note that their pool of small donors in a particular race included a surprising number of donors whose *aggregate* donations were sizeable.

Consistent with the long-standing gender difference in party preferences, compared to political donations made by men, political money coming from female donors tilts in a Democratic direction. But the gender difference among donors is not simply a matter of the disparity in partisanship. Perhaps more importantly, women donors are especially likely to direct their contributions to women candidates. Since the 1990s, Democratic female candidates for House and Senate rely most heavily – and Republican male candidates least heavily – on contributions from women (Bryner and Haley 2019; see also Thomsen and Swers 2017; Cooperman and Crowder-Meyer 2020). It is very likely that, without the willingness of women donors to support them, and organizations like EMILY'S List to fundraise for them en masse, the pattern we saw in Section 3 of increasing numbers of women, especially Democratic women, elected to Congress in recent decades would have been quite different (Delli Carpini and Fuchs 1993; Nelson 1994; Pimlott 2010).

5.2 The Gender Gap in Making Political Contributions

When we discussed Figure 3 in Section 1, we noted that only a relatively small proportion of people make any contribution at all, but that men are consistently somewhat more likely than women to make a political donation either to a political party or to an individual candidate. The gender gap was persistent for much of the period between 1964 and 2000. It closed briefly in 2004 and 2008, remerged in 2012 and 2016, and closed again in 2020. We also mentioned that rates of contributing are low for all three groups based on race or ethnicity. Furthermore, in each group in many of the years, women were somewhat less likely than men to donate. As we have seen frequently, because of the smaller sample sizes, the data are less stable for Hispanic and Black respondents.

With respect to the intersection between gender and political party, the data in Figure 24 replicate familiar patterns. In both parties, rates of donating are low and men are somewhat more likely than women to make a contribution – although the disparities on the basis of gender are greater for Democrats than Republicans.

Data about women and men in the mass public tell only a small part of the story, however. The ANES only assesses contributions to a political party or candidate and omits questions about donating to other campaign finance vehicles. Among them are political action committees (PACs), campaign finance organizations associated with, for example, a union, corporation, or trade association; and super PACs to which individuals, corporations, associations, and unions can donate unlimited sums. Super PACs are permitted to spend unlimited sums advocating for favored candidates so long as there is no

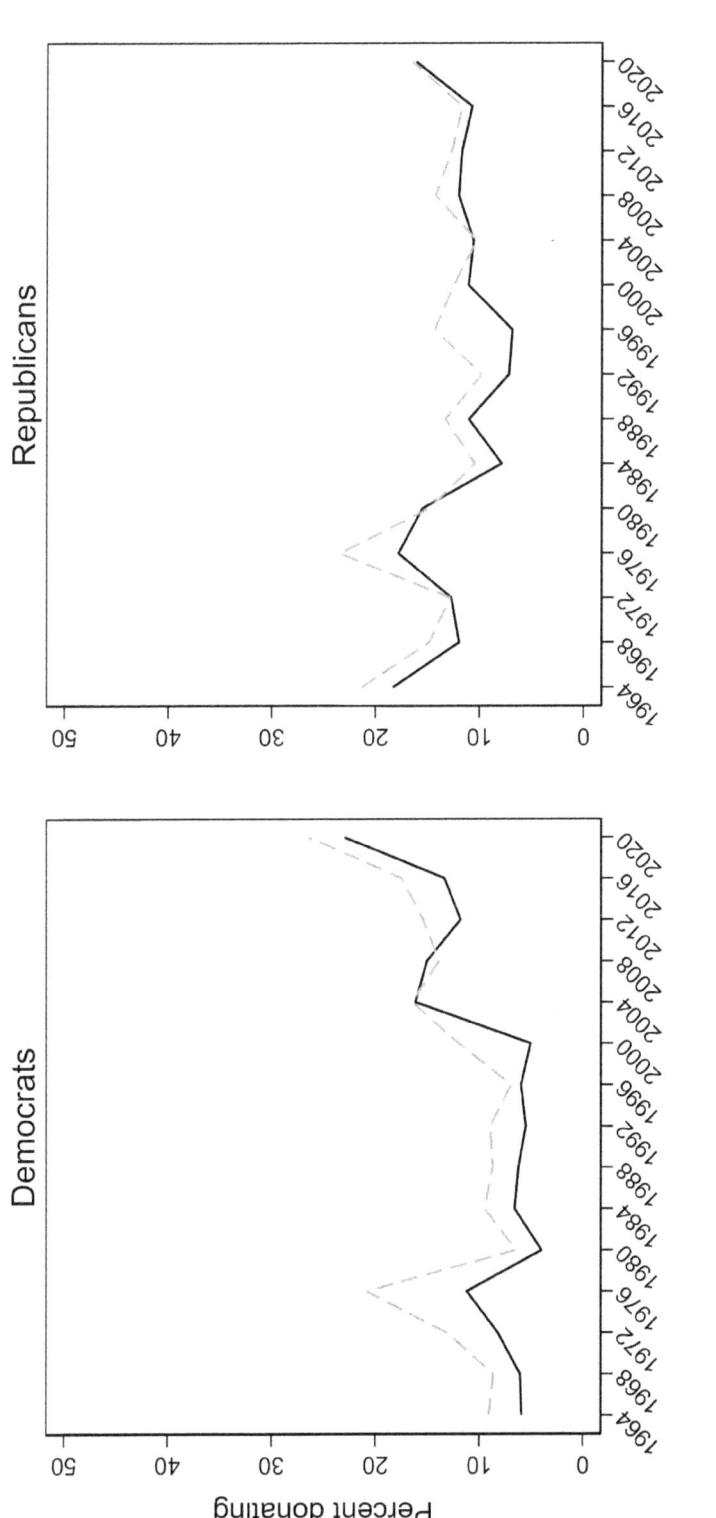

Figure 24 Percent of Democrats and Republicans donating to a political campaign by gender: 1964–2020

Data from the ANES cumulative file and the 2020 ANES (weighted).
Partisans include strong and weak partisans as well as "leaners" (independents who feel closer to one of the two parties). True Independents have been omitted.
Differences between women and men are statistically significant in the following years (bolded years at the $p<=0.05$ threshold at the $p<=0.10$ threshold) among:
Democrats: **1964**, 1972, 1976, 1992, 2000, 2012, **2016, 2020**
Republicans: **1976**, 1996

coordination between the super PAC and candidates' campaigns, a principle that may be honored in the breach. For some time, such outside spending has surpassed spending by traditional campaign organizations and PACs. Moreover, while super PACs have to disclose their donors, so-called dark money groups – which include some, but not all, kinds of nonprofits as defined by the IRS code – are not necessarily required to do so. Thus, the figures just discussed omit contributors to several kinds of campaign finance organizations, some of whom are not even known to the Federal Elections Commission.[49] Although we do not have information on donors to dark money groups, there is evidence that men are more likely than women to donate to outside organizations rather than just to candidates, parties, or PACs (OpenSecrets 2023a).

In addition, we have been focusing on contributors as individuals, irrespective of the amounts they contributed. As soon we consider the size of contributions, the narrow gaps widen. Only a small fraction of the already small fraction of American adults who make any contribution at all to a party, candidate, or PAC make contributions that require itemizing (over $200). In the 2020 election cycle, these large donors constituted less than 2 percent of American adults. Men outnumbered women in this group, constituting 55 percent of those who contributed more than $200. In addition, men's contributions were, on average, larger, accounting for 65 percent of the sums collected from such donors (OpenSecrets 2023a). In fact, regardless of party and gender, House candidates receive a larger share of their donations from men. In 2018, even Democratic women received less than a majority, 44 percent, of the contributions from women. The corresponding figure for Republican men was 23 percent (Bryner and Weber 2018). The patterns we have been discussing for national electoral patterns are replicated on the state level.[50] In state races, women are less likely to give and give, on average, smaller amounts when they contribute.

In the background of our discussion is the fact that, although the disparity in income between women and men has shrunk, it has not closed fully. Women's continuing income deficit leads us to inquire: Would the gender gap in making campaign donations disappear if women's incomes matched men's? Figure 25 presents the results of a simulation in which, for each year, we substitute for women's incomes the average income for men in that year. Figure 25 shows that equalizing incomes would raise women's rates of donating slightly but would not close the gender gap in making political contributions. Clearly, gender-based income disparities are not the whole story.

---

[49] For information on the various kinds of campaign finance organizations and the rules that govern them, see OpenSecrets 2023b.
[50] Sanbonmatsu (2023); does not include giving to PACs, SuperPACs, or dark money contributions.

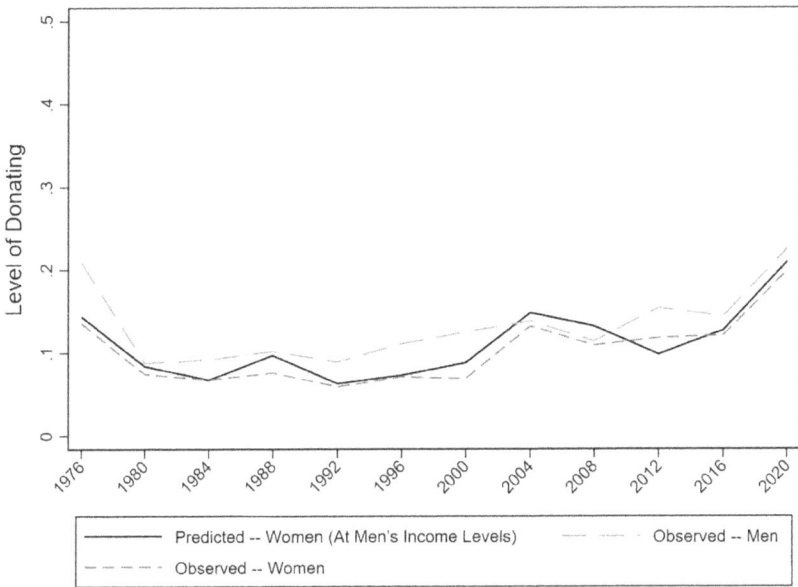

Figure 25 Observed Donating for Women and for Men vs. Predicted Donating for Women: 1976–2020
Data from the ANES cumulative file and the 2020 ANES (weighted).

5.3 Donors with Very Deep Pockets

For all the attention paid to small donors and the way that their contributions have jump-started campaigns in surprising ways, it is essential to recognize the significance of what are sometimes called "mega-donors," the deep-pocketed contributors who can make seven-figure donations. One arresting illustration of the role of very big money is that 28 percent of the identifiable individual political contributions in the 2012 election cycle came from one ten-thousandth of the U.S. population – or 1 percent of the 1 percent – a group so small that it would not fill a university football stadium (Drutman 2013).[51] Of the $45 billion in federal donations recorded between January 2009 and December 2020, an astonishing 7.5 percent came from a mere twelve donors (Beckel 2021).

To get some purchase on the representation of women and men among mega-donors, we assembled data about the fifty most generous donors in each federal election cycle between 2010 and 2020.[52] Consider Figure 26, which shows the

---

[51] This analysis seems not to have been replicated since then. (On billionaires in politics, see also Skocpol 2017; Persily, Bauer, and Ginsberg 2018; and Page, Seawright, and Lacombe 2018).

[52] The data in figures in this section were calculated by the authors from information taken from http://www.opensecrets.org. These figures do not include the large amount of so-called "dark money," which is not enumerated by the Federal Election Commission. We use data from OpenSecrets, rather than the ANES for two different reasons. As we have indicated, the ANES includes information whether a respondent donated, but not the amount of the

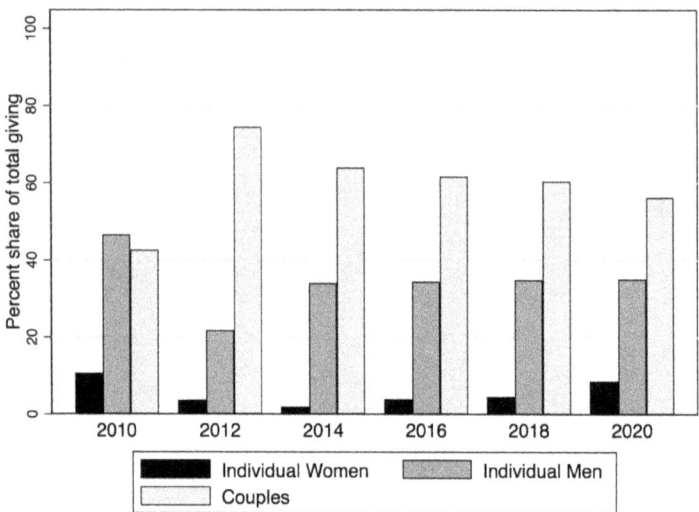

Figure 26 Share of federal dollars given to federal candidates among top 50 contributors over time, by gender and relationship status (couple or individual): 2010–2020

Data from OpenSecrets (2023a). Totals include all contributions by Top 50 Contributors to federal candidates, parties, political action committees, 527 committees, and Carey committees.

distribution of the total contributions made by these fifty fat cat donors that came from married couples, individual men, and individual women (these data include outside spending but not dark money). Note that all of the married couples in these data are heterosexual. In every year except 2010, a majority of the total contributions – which totaled nearly $1.4 billion in 2020 – was donated by married couples. Of the remainder, in each election year, contributions by individual men swamped contributions by individual women in ratios ranging from roughly 4-to-1 to 17-to-1.

Figure 27, which translates these proportions into actual dollars, shows the enormity of the sums donated by a very few people with deep pockets. Comparing presidential years with one another and off-year federal election years with one another, we see the amounts rising sharply. Not unexpectedly, in every election, total donations by individual men dwarf total donations by individual women. In short, introducing considerations of the size of donations from the most generous donors shows the modest gender gap in likelihood of

---

contribution. In addition, because such a large fraction of contributions originates with such a tiny number of people, any representative national survey, even one with a much larger sample than the ANES, would be unlikely to include many, or any, megadonors.

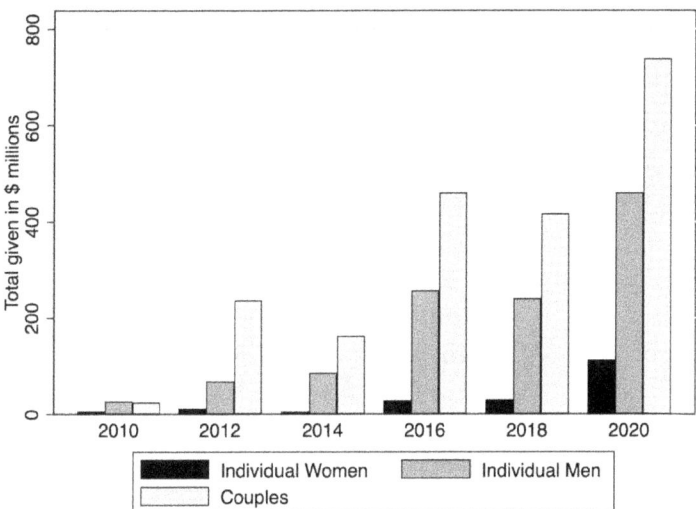

Figure 27 Total amount of dollars in millions given to federal political candidates by top 50 contributors over time, by gender and relationship status (couple or individual): 2010–2020

Data from OpenSecrets (2023a). Totals include all contributions by Top 50 Contributors to federal candidates, parties, political action committees, 527 committees, and Carey committees.

contributing to be more like a chasm. Moreover, with regard to race or ethnicity, *all* of the fifty most generous donors in 2020 were white.[53]

With respect to partisanship, although it is sometimes assumed that Republicans reap the overwhelming share of the donations from big givers, the reality is more complicated. In fact, both parties benefit from the largesse of mega-donors. Between 2010 and 2020 electoral cycles, Republicans (or conservatives) reaped 53 percent of the total contributions from the fifty most generous donors and Democrats (or liberals) 47 percent.[54] This pattern changes significantly when we consider the subgroups separately. Consistent with the fact that, in the mass public, married voters are more likely to cast Republican ballots, fully 60 percent of the aggregate 2010–2020 giving from married

---

[53] To research the race or ethnicity of big givers, we did not rely on photographs. Instead, we used whatever web sources we could locate, including the capsule biographies of the Forbes 400 in 2020: www.forbes.com/sites/chasewithorn/2020/09/08/forbes-400-2020-these-billionaires-have-gotten-the-richest-over-the-past-year/?sh=418abadb6a84. In contrast to our experience in coding the race or ethnicity of congressional candidates, we encountered few complexities or ambiguities. For a helpful review of the literature on intersectionality and campaign donations, see Grumbach, Sahn, and Staszak (2020).

[54] Although the aggregate sums are divided relatively equally between the parties, individual donors are anything but bipartisan. Not one of the top fifty donors in 2020 contributed as much as 1 percent of their total donations to the opposite party.

couples was directed to Republicans (or conservatives). For individual men and women, whose marital status is not specified, the analogous figures are 44 percent and 38 percent, respectively.

The evidence is clear. Women are unambiguously underrepresented in the class of fat-cat donors. What is less clear is why.[55] Perhaps most importantly, by a variety of measures, men's economic wherewithal surpasses women's. Men are more likely than women to be rich. On average, they earn more and are much more likely than women to be in the narrow slice of the highest earners. Besides, they command much greater wealth (Chang 2010). Notably, of the 400 wealthiest Americans listed in the Forbes 400 in 2022, all of them billionaires, only 59 were women, or about 15 percent (Forbes 2022; see also Page, Seawright, and Lacombe 2018).

Beyond gender differences in the ability to make political contributions, a number of historical, social, and psychological factors have been adduced to explain men's dominance in big-time campaign finance. One argument is that women's limited financial wherewithal leads to a sense of financial precarity which could inhibit women's financial generosity. Another is the power of the cultural legacy of the long historical period in which married women exercised little control over any financial resources they might command. Still another (Palmer and Parti 2014) is that women require a "personal touch" to be induced to give. A different approach focuses on family dynamics and the traditional view of the husband as the head of the household. However, a study of married, heterosexual couples conducted some time ago showed that, even when the members of the couple do not participate together – and they often do – they feel as if they are representing one another with their activity. Furthermore, consultation is the norm, and both halves of the couple express satisfaction with their decision-making processes. Still, according to both partners, in most couples the husband takes most of the responsibility for making financial decisions (Burns, Schlozman, and Verba 2001, chap. 12).[56]

Nevertheless, these arguments seem to be at variance with the survey-based finding from the literature on philanthropy, that with a variety of variables taken into account – including a rather crude measure of income – women are more likely than men to make charitable donations and are more generous when they give.[57]

---

[55] See, for example, contrasting arguments Palmer and Parti (2014); Traister (2014); and Walsh (2014).

[56] For a helpful examination of the array of ways households make decisions about money, see the cross-national review by Çineli (2022). In these results, which use 2012 data, 60 percent of partnered households in the United States make decisions about money jointly, 20 percent make the decisions separately and keep their money separate, and in 20 percent, only one member of the couple makes the decisions. Education is one of the strongest predictors of not using a traditional, one-person-decides system.

[57] See Mesch et al. (2011); unfortunately, the authors neither specify the variable used to measure charitable giving nor indicate what it covers. In particular, it is important to know whether

We investigated further by looking systematically at the Forbes 400, the richest individuals and families in the United States, for 2022. Profiles for each member include pertinent factoids, a "Self-Made Score" and a "Philanthropy Score" (both assigned by Forbes), and information about the person's activities including political involvements and philanthropic endeavors. What stands out is how male (86 percent) and how white (91 percent)[58] these Forbes 400 members are. Not surprisingly, these high-rollers are well represented among the biggest campaign contributors: one-third of the top 100 donors on the OpenSecrets.org listing for 2020 – including all in the top five – appear on the list of the Forbes 400. While data from the Forbes 400 about the origins of their wealth indicate that the men were much more likely than the women to be self-made, try as we might we could not find any significant gender specialization in politics or philanthropy within this group of super-rich.

Again, this appears to point to evidence of the importance of *levels* of wealth rather than *effects*. We did not find any evidence demonstrating that men in the Forbes 400 were more likely to be political donors. However, the number of white men in this group reflects that race and gender differences in who holds this level of wealth matter for demographic differences in who is a political megadonor.

Is there something special about political giving that is unattractive to women? Research about the political ambitions of students at elite institutions of higher education shows that men are systematically more likely than women to aspire to elective office. Are women perhaps simply less likely than men to see politics as useful and effective? (Shames 2015, 2017; Schneider et al. 2016). If so, why is this tendency so much more pronounced among the most affluent than among ordinary donors? Unfortunately, to the extent that these proposed explanations for the gender disparity at the highest levels of giving rest on systematic evidence – and not all of them do – the data derive from surveys of the mass public. What we know about these matters with regard to the very, very wealthy tends to be anecdotal.

5.4 Summary

This section has treated an especially consequential form of political participation that has grown substantially in recent years as a form of political input and in relative weight in the set of political activities available to American citizens. In

---

religious institutions are included. Moreover, it is unclear whether the income is individual- or family-based.

[58] Nearly two-thirds of those who are not white are Asian American. A total of seven are Black, Hispanic, or other/multiracial, which renders impossible generalizations about racial and ethnic differences within this ultra-wealthy group.

contrast to what we have seen for voting and other forms of electoral activity, the gender gap in activity has not closed for making campaign contributions. Instead, men's persistent advantage of varying size in the likelihood of making campaign donations has continued. What is more, while the gap is relatively slight among the relatively small portion of the public that makes any contribution at all, it widens among the much smaller group that makes contributions over $200. When we consider the tiny group of mega-donors – a group that accounts for an outsize share of all campaign contributions – and include contributions not only to candidates, parties, and PACs but also to outside organizations like super PACs, the dimensions of the gender gap in campaign giving seem almost unbridgeable.

6 Epilogue

What explains why, after decades in which men in the United States were consistently a bit more active in politics than women, the disparity has now mostly disappeared?

We had expected that the increasing presence of women in visible political positions and the increasing prominence in American politics of issues related to women's exclusion from and treatment in public and private life would have the consequence of selectively drawing women into politics. To our surprise and disappointment, we find that neither of these developments had the anticipated effect.

Perhaps the explanation is that the political environment does not speak for itself. The necessity of narrative is commonplace in the literature on public opinion. Facts don't speak for themselves. It may be that the presence of women in visible political roles requires narrative and interpretation; that is, it requires the dots to be connected by political movements, opinion leaders, and political and cultural interpreters. This reasoning is consistent with the pattern such that the presence of women candidates and elected officials was related to women's electoral interest during the "Year of the Woman" in 1992 and 1996, and then more faintly in 2016 and 2020.

Perhaps the explanation is that, even though issues of women's rights and roles generate intense and polarized political conflict, they do not divide women from men. In fact, despite the many gender differences in attitudes on political issues like gun rights, there is not and has not been a gender gap on what are referred to as "women's issues." (For a review of the literature, see Kinder, Reynolds, and Burns 2020.)

Perhaps the explanation is that a taste for politics is not only situational but dispositional. That is, an interest in politics can be affected by immediate political circumstances – a political scandal, an upset in a local election, a game-changing Supreme Court decision. But interest in politics is also a long-term aspect of an individual's political makeup and, thus, relatively impermeable to change, especially as the result of short-term features of the political environment (see Prior 2018; Krupnikov and Ryan 2022; Campbell and Wolbrecht 2025). Thinking of political interest as longer-term and, often, relatively stable within individuals, relating to political socialization, may help us to understand why electoral interest has responded only sporadically to the increased visibility of women and to issues related to gender in American politics. Still, the particular configuration that emerges from the data – rising levels of electoral interest for both women and men, convergence between women and men in political participation, and a consistent gender disparity in electoral interest – remains a puzzle.

Instead, the roots of the narrowing of gender disparities in political activity lie in social structural changes related to class – in particular, in women's relative gains in income and, especially, education, both of which foster participatory resources and capacities. Thus, it is not that the benefits of political action have become more obvious. It is not that women are inspired by seeing other women in politics (although for one subgroup of marginalized citizens, Black women, this does appear to make some difference). It is mostly that, as women acquire a relatively greater share of the educational and financial resources that make political work easier, the costs of participation are reduced and their political activity approaches or equals men's.

With respect to these two social-structural factors with long-established consequences for participation, what turned out to matter is changes in women's and men's relative *levels* of participatory factors rather than differences in their relative *effects* on men's and women's political activity. Women have not only closed the gender gap in college graduation, but their aggregate levels of educational attainment now surpass those of men. The story is parallel, but more muted, for income: although women have made economic progress in the past sixty years, their incomes continue to lag men's. Both income and, especially, education have a positive impact on participation, but the effects of these class-based social-structural resources on activity are no different for men than they are for women. Moreover, over time, the effects of education and income on political activity have remained more or less unchanged. Despite growing inequality, despite dramatic changes in the technologies around activism, despite the polarization of the electorate, the relationship between these two resources and political activity has hardly varied.

While disparities on the basis of gender in voting turnout and campaign participation have closed, from one perspective men's advantage in making political donations has probably become more pronounced. In our era of free-for-all campaign finance, the sums given to political candidates and causes have skyrocketed. Because men are much more likely than women to command enormous financial resources, when we focus on the number of dollars rather than on the number of donors, the gender disparity in political giving has widened.

With respect to groups defined by the intersection of gender and race or ethnicity, we noted differences among the six groups in the social-structural variables that function so critically in facilitating participation. White Americans enjoy higher levels of both education and income than do Black or Hispanic Americans. Over time, educational attainment has risen for all three groups. Within each group, however, the educational gains have been greater for women than for men, a reversal that happened first for Black Americans, then for Hispanic Americans, and later for white Americans. Average weekly wages are higher for white Americans than for other groups. In each group, there is a gender wage gap – widest for white Americans, narrowest for Black Americans – that has diminished over time. Still, in none of these groups have women overtaken men when it comes to earnings. And looking at command over wealth such as property-owning shows gender disparities favoring men in each racial and ethnic group, widest among white Americans but still substantial for Black and Hispanic Americans (Chang 2010; Kent 2021).

In view of the role played by both education and income in political participation, the intersectional disparities in political activity derive, at least in part, from group differences in social-structural resources. We must re-emphasize a point raised in the introduction. The ability to account for participatory differences among groups defined by gender and race or ethnicity on the basis of other variables does not render irrelevant these group identities. Group differences in average education and income are not simply coincidental. Instead, they reflect socially structured experiences intimately connected to group membership. And whatever their origins, the differences in political activity among intersectionally defined groups mean that public officials hear much more from some people – and some kinds of people – than from others.

This meditation on unequal participation brings us full circle back to the "gender gap" as it is usually construed – that is, the aggregate differences between women and men in vote choices, party identification, and attitudes on certain public issues. Not only do women and men differ in their political opinions and choices but the six intersectional groups can be further differentiated by their distinctive politically relevant characteristics. When those who speak with a megaphone – or who make huge campaign donations – differ in their political preferences and needs for government policy from those who speak in a whisper, the democratic promise of equal responsiveness to all citizens is in jeopardy.

References

Aldrich, J. H., and McGraw, K. M. (2011). *Improving Public Opinion Surveys: Interdisciplinary Innovation and the ANES*. Princeton: Princeton University Press.

Atkeson, L. R., and Carrillo, N. (2007). More is Better: The Influence of Collective Female Descriptive Representation on External Efficacy. *Politics & Gender* 3(1), 79–101.

Autor, D., Figlio, D., Karbownik, K., Roth, J., and Wasserman, M. (2019). Family Disadvantage and the Gender Gap in Behavioral and Educational Outcomes. *American Economic Journal: Applied Economics* 11(3), 338–381.

Barreto, M. A. (2007). ¡Sí Se Puede! Latino Candidates and the Mobilization of Latino Voters. *American Political Science Review* 101(3), 425–441.

Barreto, M. A. (2010). *Ethnic Cues: The Role of Shared Ethnicity in Latino Political Participation*. Ann Arbor: University of Michigan Press.

Barreto, M. A., Segura, G. M., and Woods, N. D. (2004). The Mobilizing Effect of Majority–Minority Districts on Latino Turnout. *American Political Science Review* 98(1), 65–75.

Barreto, M. A., Frasure-Yokley, L., Vargas, E. D., and Wong, J. (2018). Best Practices in Collecting Online Data with Asian, Black, Latino, and White Respondents. *Politics, Groups, and Identities* 6(1), 171–180.

Baxter, S., and Lansing, M. (1983). *The Invisible Majority*. Ann Arbor: University of Michigan Press.

Beaman, L., Duflo, E., Pande, R., and Topalova, P. (2012). Female Leadership Raises Aspirations and Educational Attainment for Girls: A Policy Experiment in India. *Science* 335(6068), 582–586.

Beckel, M. (2021). Outsize Influence, Issue One. https://issueone.org/articles/outsized-influence-12-political-megadonors-are-responsible-for-1-of-every-13-in-federal-elections-since-citizens-united-and-25-of-all-giving-from-the-top-100-zip-codes-a-total-of-3-4-bil/.

Bejarano, C. (2013). *The Latina Gender Gap in U.S. Politics*. New York: Routledge.

Berent, M. K., Krosnick, J. A., and Lupia, A. (2016). Measuring Voter Registration and Turnout in Surveys: Do Official Government Records Yield More Accurate Assessments? *Public Opinion Quarterly* 80(3), 597–621.

Berinsky, A. J., and Lenz, G. S. (2011). Education and Political Participation: Exploring the Causal Link. *Political Behavior* 33(3), 357–373.

Bernhard, R., Shames, S., and Teele, D. (2021). To Emerge? Breadwinning, Motherhood, and Women's Decisions to Run for Office. *American Political Science Review* 115(2), 379–394.

Blackburn, R. M., Jarman, J., and Racko, G. (2016). Understanding Gender Inequality in Employment and Retirement. *Contemporary Social Science* 11 (2–3), 238–252.

Blais, A., and Achen, C. H. (2019). Civic Duty and Voter Turnout. *Political Behavior* 41(2), 473–497.

Blau, F. D., and Kahn, L. M. (2007). The Gender Pay Gap: Have Women Gone as Far as They Can? *Academy of Management Perspectives* 21(1), 7–23.

Blau, F. D., and Kahn, L. M. (2017). The Gender Wage Gap: Extent, Trends, and Explanations. *Journal of Economic Literature* 55(3), 789–865.

Blau, F. D., Brinton, F. D., and Grusky, D. B., eds. (2006). *The Declining Significance of Gender?* New York: Russell Sage Foundation.

Boatright, R., and Sperling, V. (2020). *Trumping Politics as Usual*. New York: Oxford University Press.

Bobo, L., and Gilliam Jr., F. D. (1990). Race, Sociopolitical Participation and Empowerment. *American Political Science Review* 84(2), 377–393.

Bos, A. L., Greenlee, J. S., Holman, M. R., Oxley, Z. M., and Lay, J. C. (2022). This One's for the Boys: How Gendered Political Socialization Limits Girls' Political Ambition and Interest. *American Political Science Review* 116(2), 484–501.

Box-Steffensmeier, J. M. (1996). A Dynamic Analysis of the Role of War Chests in Campaign Strategy. *American Journal of Political Science* 40(2), 352–371.

Box-Steffensmeier, J. M., De Boef, S., and Lin, T. (2004). The Dynamics of the Partisan Gender Gap. *American Political Science Review* 98(3), 515–528.

Brady, H. E. (1999). Political Participation. In *Measures of Political Attitudes*, Vol. 2, Robinson, J. P., Shaver, P. R., and Wrightsman, L. S., eds. Cambridge: Academic Press, 737–801.

Brown, N. E. (2014). Political Participation of Women of Color: An Intersectional Analysis. *Journal of Women, Politics & Policy* 35(4), 315–348.

Brown, N. E., and Gershon, S. A. (2016). *Distinct Identities: Minority Women in U.S. Politics*. New York: Routledge.

Brown, N. E., and Lemi, D. C. (2020). "Life for Me Ain't Been No Crystal Stair": Black Women Candidates and the Democratic Party. *Boston University Law Review* 100, 1611–1634.

Browning, R. P., Marshall, D. R., and Tabb, D. H. (1984). *Protest Is Not Enough: The Struggle of Blacks and Hispanics for Equity in Urban Politics*. Berkeley: University of California Press.

Browning, R. P., Marshall, D. R., and Tabb, D. H. (1986). Protest Is Not Enough: A Theory of Political Incorporation. *PS: Political Science and Politics* 19(3), 576–581.

Bryner, S., and Haley, G. (2019). Race, Gender, and Money in Politics. Peter G. Peterson Foundation, March 15. www.pgpf.org/us-2050/research-projects/Race-Gender-and-Money-in-Politics-Campaign-Finance-and-Federal-Candidates-in-the-2018-Midterms/.

Bryner, S., and Weber, D. (2013). Sex, Money and Politics. Report for OpenSecrets/Center for Responsive Politics. www.opensecrets.org/news/reports/sex-money-politics.

Bryner, S., and Weber, D. (2018). Women March onto the Ballot in 2018. Report for OpenSecrets/Center for Responsive Politics. www.opensecrets.org/news/reports/women-candidates/.

Burns, N., and Gallagher, K. (2010). Public Opinion on Gender Issues: The Politics of Equity and Roles. *Annual Review of Political Science* 13, 425–443.

Burns, N., and Jardina, A. (2016). Advances and Ambivalence: The Consequences of Women's Educational and Workforce Changes for Women's Political Participation in the U.S., 1952 to 2012. In *A Half Century of Change in the Lives of American Women*, Bailey, M., and DiPrete, T., eds. New York: Russell Sage Foundation, 272–301.

Burns, N., Jardina, A, and Yadon, N. (2017). Women as a Force in Electoral Politics. In *The Oxford Handbook of U.S. Women's Social Movement Activism*, McCammon, H. J., Banaszak, L. A., Taylor, V., and Reger, J., eds. New York: Oxford University Press, 507–521.

Burns, N., Schlozman, K. L., and Verba, S. (2001). *The Private Roots of Public Action*. Cambridge, MA: Harvard University Press.

Burns, N., Schlozman, K., Jardina, A., Shames, S., and Verba, S. (2018). What's Happened to the Gender Gap in Political Participation? In *100 Years of the Nineteenth Amendment: An Appraisal of Women's Political Activism*, McCammon, H. J., and Banaszak, L. A., eds. New York: Oxford University Press, 69–104.

Calhoun-Brown, A. (1996). African American Churches and Political Mobilization: The Psychological Impact of Organizational Resources. *The Journal of Politics* 58(4), 935–953.

Campaign Finance Institute. (2023). Analyses of Campaign Finance Data. www.cfinst.org/data.aspx.

References

Campbell, D. E. (2016). Doing the Lord's Work: How Religious Congregations Build Civic Skills. In *New Advances in the Study of Civic Voluntarism*, Klofstad, C. A., ed. Philadelphia: Temple University Press.

Campbell, D. E., and Wolbrecht, C. (2006). See Jane Run: Women Politicians as Role Models for Adolescents. *The Journal of Politics* 68(2), 233–247.

Campbell, D. E., and Wolbrecht, C. (2025). *See Jane Run: How Women Politicians Matter for Young People*. Chicago: University of Chicago Press.

Carnes, N. (2013). *White-Collar Government: The Hidden Role of Class in Economic Policy Making*. Chicago: University of Chicago Press.

Cassese, E. C., and Holman, M. R. (2019). Playing the Woman Card: Ambivalent Sexism in the 2016 US Presidential Race. *Political Psychology* 40(1), 55–74.

Cassese, E. C., Barnes, T. D., and Branton, R. P. (2015). Racializing Gender: Public Opinion at the Intersection. *Politics & Gender* 11(1), 1–26.

Cassese, E. C., Bos, A. L., and Schneider, M. C. (2014). Whose American Government? A Quantitative Analysis of Gender and Authorship in American Politics Texts. *Journal of Political Science Education* 10(3), 253–272.

CAWP (2023a). Gender Gap. Report by the Center for American Women and Politics, New Brunswick, NJ. https://cawp.rutgers.edu/facts/voters/gender-gap.

CAWP (2023b). Gender Differences in Voter Turnout. Report by the Center for American Women and Politics, New Brunswick, NJ. https://cawp.rutgers.edu/facts/voters/gender-differences-voter-turnout#GGN.

CAWP (2023c). Women Officeholders by Race and Ethnicity. Report by the Center for American Women and Politics, New Brunswick, NJ. https://cawp.rutgers.edu/facts/voters/gender-differences-voter-turnout#GGN.

Chan, N. K., and Phoenix, D. L. (2020). The Ties that Bind: Assessing the Effects of Political and Racial Church Homogeneity on Asian American Political Participation. *Politics and Religion* 13(3), 639–670.

Chang, M. L. (2010). *Shortchanged: Why Women Have Less Wealth and What Can Be Done about It*. New York: Oxford University Press.

Chenoweth, E., and Pressman, J. (2017). This Is What We Learned by Counting the Women's Marches. *The Washington Post*, February 7. www.washingtonpost.com/news/monkey-cage/wp/2017/02/07/this-is-what-we-learned-by-counting-the-womens-marches/.

Chong, D., and Rogers, R. (2005). Racial Solidarity and Political Participation. *Political Behavior* 27(4), 347–374.

Çineli, B. (2022). Who Manages the Money at Home? Multilevel Analysis of Couples' Money Management across 34 Countries. *Gender & Society* 36(1), 32–62.

Clark, C. J. (2014). Collective Descriptive Representation and Black Voter Mobilization in 2008. *Political Behavior* 36(2), 315–333.

Clayton, A., O'Brien, D. Z., and Piscopo, J. M. (2019). All Male Panels? Representation and Democratic Legitimacy. *American Journal of Political Science* 63(1), 113–129.

Cleveland, J. N., Stockdale, M., and Murphy, K. R. (2000). *Women & Men in Organizations: Sex and Gender Issues at Work*. Mahwah: Lawrence Erlbaum Associates.

Cole, E. R., and Stewart, A. J. (1996). Meanings of Political Participation among Black and White Women: Political Identity and Social Responsibility. *Journal of Personality and Social Psychology* 71(1), 130–140.

Combahee River Collective. (1977). Statement of the Combahee River Collective. In *Feminism in Our Time: The Essential Writings, World War II to the Present*, Schneir, M., ed. New York: Vintage Books.

Conley, D. (2010). *Being Black, Living in the Red: Race, Wealth, and Social Policy in America*. Berkeley: University of California Press.

Cooperman, R., and Crowder-Meyer, M. (2020). Standing on Their Shoulders: Suffragists, Women's PACs, and Demands for Women's Representation. *PS: Political Science and Politics* 53(3), 470–473.

Crenshaw, K. (1990). Mapping the Margins: Intersectionality, Identity Politics, and Violence against Women of Color. *Stanford Law Review* 43, 1241–1299.

Dalton, R. J. (2017). *The Participation Gap: Social Status and Political Inequality*. New York: Oxford University Press.

Dalton, R. J., and Klingemann, H.-D, eds. (2007). *The Oxford Handbook of Political Behavior*. Oxford Handbooks, Part VI, 621–799.

Dawson, M. C. (1994). *Behind the Mule: Race and Class in African-American Politics*. Princeton: Princeton University Press.

de la Garza, R. O., and DeSipio, L. (1993). Save the Baby, Change the Bathwater, and Scrub the Tub: Latino Electoral Participation after Seventeen Years of Voting Rights Act Coverage. *Texas Law Review* 71(7), 1479–1540.

Delli Carpini, M. X., and Fuchs, E. R. (1993). The Year of the Woman? Candidates, Voters, and the 1992 Elections. *Political Science Quarterly* 108(1), 29–36.

Dinesen, P. T., Dawes, C. T., Johannesson, M., Klemmensen, R ; Magnusson, P., Nørgaard, A.S., Petersen, I., and Oskarsson, S. (2016). Estimating the Impact of Education on Political Participation: Evidence from Monozygotic Twins in the U.S., Denmark and Sweden. *Political Behavior* 38(3), 579–601.

DiPrete, T. A., and Buchmann, C. (2013). *The Rise of Women: The Growing Gender Gap in Education and What it Means for American Schools.* New York: Russell Sage Foundation.

Dittmar, K. (2016). Finding Gender in Election 2016. Center for American Women and Politics. https://cawp.rutgers.edu/sites/default/files/resources/presidential-gender-gap_report_final.pdf.

Dittmar, K. (2021). Reaching Higher: Black Women in American Politics 2021. Center for American Women and Politics. https://cawp.rutgers.edu/sites/default/files/2021-2/black_women_in_politics_2021_1.pdf.

Dittmar, K. (2022). Latinas in U.S. Politics 2022. Center for American Women and Politics. https://latinasrepresent.org/reports/.

Dolan, K. (2006). Symbolic Mobilization? The Impact of Candidate Sex in American Elections. *American Politics Research* 34(6), 687–704.

Dowe, P. K. F. (2020). Resisting Marginalization: Black Women's Political Ambition and Agency. *PS: Political Science and Politics* 53(4), 697–702.

Drutman, L. (2013). The Political 1% of the 1% in 2012. Report for the Sunlight Foundation. June 24. https://sunlightfoundation.com/2013/06/24/1pct_of_the_1pct/.

Elder, L. (2021). *The Partisan Gap: Why Democratic Women Get Elected but Republican Women Don't.* New York: New York University Press.

Farris, E. M., and Holman, M. R. (2014). Social Capital and Solving the Puzzle of Black Women's Political Participation. *Politics, Groups, and Identities* 2(3), 331–349.

Forbes. (2022). The Forbes 400: The Definitive Ranking of the Wealthiest Americans in 2022. www.forbes.com/forbes-400/.

Fraga, B. L. (2018). *The Turnout Gap: Race, Ethnicity, and Political Inequality in a Diversifying America.* New York: Cambridge University Press.

Gay, C. (2001). The Effect of Black Congressional Representation on Political Participation. *American Political Science Review* 95(3), 589–602.

Gay, C. (2002). Spirals of Trust? The Effect of Descriptive Representation on the Relationship between Citizens and their Government. *American Journal of Political Science* 46(4), 717–733.

Gay, C., and Tate, K. (1998). Doubly Bound: The Impact of Gender and Race on the Politics of Black Women. *Political Psychology* 19(1), 169–184.

Gerber, A. S. (2004). Does Campaign Spending Work? Field Experiments Provide Evidence and Suggest New Theory. *American Behavioral Scientist* 47(5), 541–574.

Gerber, A. S., Huber, G. A., Doherty, D., Dowling, C.M. ; Raso, C. ; and Ha, S. E. (2011). Personality Traits and Participation in Political Processes. *Journal of Politics* 73(3), 692–706.

Gillespie, A., and Brown, N. E. (2019). #BlackGirlMagic Demystified. *Phylon* 56(2), 37–58.

Glynn, S. J. (2019). Breadwinning Mothers Continue to Be the U.S. Norm. Center for American Progress. www.americanprogress.org/article/breadwinning-mothers-continue-u-s-norm/.

Grasso, M., and Smith, K. (2022). Gender Inequalities in Political Participation and Political Engagement among Young People in Europe. *Politics* 42(1), 39–57.

Green, D. P., and Gerber, A. S. (2019). *Get out the Vote: How to Increase Voter Turnout*. 4th ed. Washington, DC: Brookings Institution Press.

Griffin, J. D., and Keane, M. (2006). Descriptive Representation and the Composition of African-American Turnout. *American Journal of Political Science* 50(4), 998–1012.

Grumbach, J. M., Sahn, A., and Staszak, S. (2020). Gender, Race, and Intersectionality in Campaign Finance. *Political Behavior* 44, 1–22.

Hancock, A.-M. (2016.) *Intersectionality: An Intellectual History*. New York: Oxford University Press.

Harris, F., Chapman, V., and McKenzie, B. D. (2005). Macrodynamics of Black Political Participation in the Post-Civil Rights Era. *Journal of Politics* 67(4), 1143–1163.

Hauser, R. M. (1993). Trends in College Entry among Whites, Blacks, and Hispanics. In *Studies of Supply and Demand in Higher Education*, Clotfelter, C. T., and Rothschild, M., eds. Chicago: University of Chicago Press, 61–120.

Hellevik, O. (2009). Linear versus Logistic Regression when the Dependent Variable Is a Dichotomy. *Quality and Quantity* 41(1), 59–74.

Henderson, J. A., Sekhon, J. S., and Titiunik, R. (2016). Cause or Effect? Turnout in Hispanic Majority-Minority Districts. *Political Analysis* 24(3), 404–412.

Herrick, R., and Mendez, J. M. (2019). One Model Does Not Fit All: Group Consciousness and the Political Participation and Attitudes of American Indians. *Social Science Quarterly* 100(5), 1577–1592.

Hersh, E. D., and Schaffner, B. F. (2017). Motivations of Political Contributors: An Audit. Working Paper, Bipartisan Policy Center, Washington, DC.

Hinojosa, M. (2012). *Selecting Women, Electing Women: Political Representation and Candidate Selection in Latin America*. Philadelphia: Temple University Press.

Hinojosa, M., and Kittilson, M. C. (2020). *Seeing Women, Strengthening Democracy: How Women in Politics Foster Connected Citizens*. New York: Oxford University Press.

Holbein, J. B. (2017). Childhood Skill Development and Adult Political Participation. *American Political Science Review* 111(3), 572–583.

Holman, M. R. (2016). The Differential Effect of Resources on Political Participation across Gender and Racial Groups. In *Distinct Identities*, Brown, N., and Gershon, S. A., eds. New York: Routledge, 29–44.

hooks, b. (1981). *Ain't I a Woman? Black Women and Feminism*. Boston: South End Press.

Houston, W. W. (2013). Women Breadwinners: The Natural Order. *The Economist*, May 31. www.economist.com/democracy-in-america/2013/05/31/the-natural-order.

Huyser K. R., Sanchez G. R., and Vargas, E. D. (2017). Civic Engagement and Political Participation among American Indians and Alaska Natives in the U.S. *Politics, Groups, and Identities* 5(4), 642–659.

Igielnik, R, Keeter, S., Kennedy, C., and Spahn, B. (2018). Commercial Voter Files and the Study of U.S. Politics. Pew Research Center. www.pewresearch.org/methods/2018/02/15/commercial-voter-files-and-the-study-of-u-s-politics/.

Jackman, S., and Spahn, B. (2019). Why Does the ANES Overestimate Voter Turnout? *Political Analysis* 27(2), 193–207.

Jacob, A. G. (2006). Asian American Political Participation: Research Challenges for an Emerging Minority. *PS: Political Science and Politics* 39(1): 103–106.

Jacobs, L. R., Cook, F. L., and Delli Carpini, M. X. (2009). *Talking Together: Public Deliberation and Political Participation in America*. Chicago: University of Chicago Press.

Jacobson, G. C. (2006). Campaign Spending Effects in U.S. Senate Elections: Evidence from the National Annenberg Election Survey. *Electoral Studies* 25(2), 195–226.

Jardina, A., and Ollerenshaw, T. (2022). Poll Trends: The Polarization of White Racial Attitudes and Support for Racial Equality in the U.S. *Public Opinion Quarterly* 86(S1), 576–587.

Jenkins, C., White, I., Hanmer, M., and Banks, A. (2021). Vote Overreporting While Black: Identifying the Mechanism behind Black Survey Respondents' Vote Overreporting. *American Politics Research* 49(5), 439–451.

Junn, J. (1991). Participation and Political Knowledge. In *Political Participation and American Democracy*, Crotty, W., ed. Westport: Greenwood Press, 193–212.

Junn, J., and Brown, N. (2008). What Revolution? Incorporating Intersectionality in Women and Politics. In *Political Women and American Democracy*, Wolbrecht, C., Beckwith, K., and Baldez, L., eds. New York: Cambridge University Press, 64–78.

Junn, J., and Masuoka, N. (2008). Asian American Identity: Shared Racial Status and Political Context. *Perspectives on Politics* 6(4), 729–740.

Junn, J., and Masuoka, N. (2020). The Gender Gap is a Race Gap: Women Voters in U.S. Presidential Elections. *Perspectives on Politics* 18(4), 1135–1145.

Kam, C. D., and Palmer, C. L. (2008). Reconsidering the Effects of Education on Political Participation. *The Journal of Politics* 70(3), 612–631.

Keele, L., and White, I. (2011). African-American Turnout in Majority Minority Districts. Paper Presented at the American Political Science Association Annual Meeting, Seattle, WA.

Kent, A. H. (2021). Gender Wealth Gaps in the U.S. and Benefits of Closing Them. Federal Reserve Bank of St. Louis Blog. September 29. www.stlouisfed.org/open-vault/2021/september/gender-wealth-gaps-us-benefits-of-closing-them.

Killewald, A., Pfeffer, F. T., and Schachner, J. N. (2017). Wealth Inequality and Accumulation. *Annual Review of Sociology* 43, 379–404.

Kim, C., and Junn, J. (2024). Whitewashing Women Voters: Intersectionality and Partisan Vote Choice in the 2020 US Presidential Election. *Politics & Gender [firstview]*; 1–26.

Kinder, D. R., and Chudy, J. (2016). After Obama. *The Forum* 14(1), 3–15.

Kinder, D. R., and Sanders, L. M. (1996). *Divided by Color: Racial Politics and Democratic Ideals*. Chicago: University of Chicago Press.

Kinder, D., Reynolds, M., and Burns, N. (2020). Categorical Politics in Action: Gender and the 2016 Presidential Election. In *New Directions in Public Opinion*, Berinsky, A., ed., 3rd ed. New York: Routledge, 159–176.

Klar, S. (2018). When Common Identities Decrease Trust: An Experimental Study of Partisan Women. *American Journal of Political Science* 62(3), 610–622.

Krupnikov, Y., and Levine, A. S. (2016). Psyched about Participation. In *New Advances in the Study of Civic Voluntarism*, Klofstad, C. A., ed. Philadelphia: Temple University Press, 179–195.

Krupnikov, Y., and Ryan, J. B. (2022.) *The Other Divide: Polarization and Disagreement in American Politics*. New York: Cambridge University Press.

Laurison, D., Brown, H., and Rastogi, A. (2022). Voting Intersections: Race, Class, and Participation in Presidential Elections in the U.S. 2008–2016. *Sociological Perspectives* 65(4), 768–789.

Lawless, J. L. (2004). Politics of Presence: Congresswomen and Symbolic Representation. *Political Research Quarterly* 57(1), 81–99.

Lawless, J. L., and Fox, R. L. (2015). *Running from Office: Why Young Americans are Turned off to Politics*. New York: Oxford University Press.

Leighley, J. E. (1995). Attitudes, Opportunities, and Incentives: A Field Essay on Political Participation. *Political Research Quarterly* 48(1), 181–209.

Leighley, J. E., ed. (2010). *The Oxford Handbook of American Elections and Political Behavior*. New York: Oxford University Press.

Leighley, J. E., and Nagler, J. (2014). *Who Votes Now? Demographics, Issues, Inequality, and Turnout in the U.S.* Princeton: Princeton University Press.

Lemi, D. C. (2021). Do Voters Prefer Just Any Descriptive Representative? The Case of Multiracial Candidates. *Perspectives on Politics* 19(4), 1061–1081.

Lien, P.-T. (1994). Ethnicity and Political Participation: A Comparison between Asian and Mexican Americans. *Political Behavior* 16(2), 237–264.

Lien, P.-T. (1998). Does the Gender Gap in Political Attitudes and Behavior Vary across Racial Groups? *Political Research Quarterly* 51(4): 869–894.

Lien, P.-T. (2001). *The Making of Asian America through Political Participation*. Philadelphia: Temple University Press.

Lien, P.-T., Collet, C., Wong, J., and Ramakrishnan, S. K. (2001). Asian Pacific-American Public Opinion and Political Participation. *PS: Political Science and Politics* 34(3), 625–630.

Lizotte, M.-K. (2020). *Gender Differences in Public Opinion: Values and Political Consequences*. Philadelphia: Temple University Press.

MacManus, S. A., Bullock, C. S., and Grothe, B. P. (1986). A Longitudinal Examination of Political Participation Rates of Mexican American Females. *Social Science Quarterly* 67(3), 604–612.

Mangum, M. (2003). Psychological Involvement and Black Voter Turnout. *Political Research Quarterly* 56(1), 41–48.

Mariani, M., Marshall, B. W., and Mathews-Schultz, A. L. (2015). See Hillary Clinton, Nancy Pelosi, and Sarah Palin Run? Party, Ideology, and the Influence of Female Role Models on Young Women. *Political Research Quarterly* 68(4), 716–731.

Massey, D., Charles, C. Z., Lundy, G., and Fischer, M. J. (2006). *The Source of the River: The Social Origins of Freshmen at America's Selective Colleges and Universities*. Princeton: Princeton University Press.

Masuoka, N. (2008). Defining the Group: Latino Identity and Political Participation. *American Politics Research* 36(1), 33–61.

Masuoka, N., Ramanathan, K., and Junn, J. (2019). New Asian American Voters: Political Incorporation and Participation in 2016. *Political Research Quarterly* 72(4), 991–1003.

Maxwell, A., and Shields, T. (2017). The Impact of "Modern Sexism" on the 2016 Presidential Election. Diane D. Blair Center for Southern Politics & Society. blaircenter.uark.edu/the-impact-of-modern-sexism/.

McDaniel, A., DiPrete, T. A., Buchmann, C., and Shwed, U. (2011). The Black Gender Gap in Educational Attainment: Historical Trends and Racial Comparisons. *Demography* 48(3), 889–914.

McDonald, M. P. (2007). The True Electorate: A Cross-Validation of Voter Registration Files and Election Survey Demographics. *Public Opinion Quarterly* 71(4), 588–602.

Mesch, D. J., Brown, M., Moore, Z., and Hayat, A. (2011). Gender Differences in Charitable Giving. *International Journal of Nonprofit and Voluntary Sector Marketing* 16(4), 291–297.

Micheletti, M., and McFarland, A. eds. (2010). *Creative Participation: Responsibility-Taking in the Political World*. Boulder: Paradigm.

Milbrath, L. W., and Goel, M. L. (1977). *Political Participation*, 2nd ed. Chicago: Rand McNally.

Montoya, L. (1997). Investigating Latino Gender Differences in Political Participation. Presented at the Annual Meeting of the American Political Science Association, Washington, DC.

Montoya, L. (2000). Gender and Citizenship in Latino Political Participation. Presented at the Conference on Latinos in the 21st Century: The Research Agenda. David Rockefeller Center for Latin American Studies, Harvard University, Cambridge, MA.

Montoya, L., Hardy-Fanta, C., and Garcia, S. (2000). Latina Politics: Gender, Participation, and Leadership. *PS: Political Science and Politics* 33(3), 555–561.

Murphy, E., and Oesch, D. (2016). The Feminization of Occupations and Changes in Wages: A Panel Analysis of Britain, Germany, and Switzerland. *Social Forces* 94(3), 1221–1255.

Nelson, C. J. (1994). Women's PACs in the Year of the Woman (Chap. 10). In *The Year of the Woman: Myths and Realities*, Cook, E. A, Thomas, S., and Wilcox, C., eds. New York: Routledge, 181–196.

Nie, N. H., Junn, J., and Stehlik-Barry, K. (1996). *Education and Democratic Citizenship in America*. Chicago: University of Chicago Press.

Norris, P., and van Es, A. A., eds. (2016). *Checkbook Elections? Political Finance in Comparative Perspective*. New York: Oxford University Press.

Oliver, S., and Conroy, M. (2020). *Who Runs? The Masculine Advantage in Candidate Emergence*. Ann Arbor: University of Michigan Press.

Ondercin, H. L. (2022). Location, Location, Location: How Electoral Opportunities Shape Women's Emergence as Candidates. *The British Journal of Political Science* 52(4), 1523–1543.

OpenSecrets. (2023a). Who Are the Biggest Donors? www.opensecrets.org/elections-overview/biggest-donors.

OpenSecrets. (2023b). Dark Money Basics. www.opensecrets.org/dark-money/basics.
Page, B. I., Seawright, J., and Lacombe, M. J. (2018). *Billionaires and Stealth Politics*. Chicago: University of Chicago Press.
Palmer, A., and Parti, T. (2014). Money Gap: Why Don't Women Give? *Politico*, July 22. www.politico.com/story/2014/07/women-political-donations-109206.
Palmer, B., and Simon, D. (2006). *Breaking the Political Glass Ceiling: Women and Congressional Elections*. New York: Routledge.
Palmer, B., and Simon, D. (2012). *Women and Congressional Elections: A Century of Change*. Boulder: Lynne Rienner.
Pantoja, A. D., Ramirez, R., and Segura, G. M. (2001). Citizens by Choice, Voters by Necessity: Patterns in Political Mobilization by Naturalized Latinos. *Political Research Quarterly* 54(4), 729–750.
Persily, N., Bauer, R. F., and Ginsberg, B. L. (2018). Campaign Finance in the U.S.: Assessing an Era of Fundamental Change. Report for the Bipartisan Policy Center, Washington, DC. https://bipartisanpolicy.org/report/the-state-of-campaign-finance/.
Peterson, G. (1997). Native American Turnout in the 1990 and 1992 Elections. *American Indian Quarterly* 21(2), 321–331.
Pettit, B. (2012). *Invisible Men: Mass Incarceration and the Myth of Black Progress*. New York: Russell Sage Foundation.
Pew Research. (2013). Breadwinner Moms. www.pewresearch.org/social-trends/2013/05/29/breadwinner-moms/.
Pew Research. (2022). For Many U.S. Moms, Pandemic Brought Increase in Time Spent Caring for Kids While Doing Other Things. www.pewresearch.org/short-reads/2022/10/11/for-many-u-s-moms-pandemic-brought-increase-in-time-spent-caring-for-kids-while-doing-other-things/.
Phillips, C. D., and Lee, T. (2018). Superficial Equality: Gender and Immigration in Asian American Political Participation. *Politics, Groups, and Identities* 6(3), 373–388.
Philpot, T. S., and Walton, H., Jr. (2007). One of Our Own: Black Female Candidates and the Voters Who Support Them. *American Journal of Political Science* 51(1), 49–62.
Philpot, T. S., and Walton, H., Jr. (2014). African American Political Participation. In *The Oxford Handbook of Racial and Ethnic Politics in the U.S.*, Leal, D. L., Lee, T., and Sawyer, M., eds. New York: Oxford University Press, 1–12. https://academic.oup.com/edited-volume/41327/chapter/497000178.

Philpot, T. S., Shaw, D. R., and McGowen, E. B. (2009). Winning the Race: Black Voter Turnout in the 2008 Presidential Election. *Public Opinion Quarterly* 73(5), 995–1022.

Pimlott, J. P. (2010). *Women and the Democratic Party: The Evolution of Emily's List.* Amherst, NY: Cambria Press.

Presser, S., and Traugott, M. (1992). Little White Lies and Social Science Models: Correlated Response Errors in a Panel Study of Voting. *Public Opinion Quarterly* 56(1), 77–86.

Prior, M. (2018). *Hooked: How Politics Captures People's Interest.* New York: Cambridge University Press.

Ramakrishnan, S. K., and Bloemraad, I., eds. (2008). *Civic Hopes and Political Realities: Immigrants, Community Organizations, and Political Engagement.* New York: Russell Sage Foundation.

Ramakrishnan, S. K., Lee, J., Lee, T., and Wong, J. (2008). National Asian American Survey (NAAS) Riverside, CA: National Asian American Survey (archived at ICPSR, University of Michigan).

Ramakrishnan, S. K., Lee, J., Lee, T., and Wong, J. (2016). National Asian American Survey (NAAS) Riverside, CA: National Asian American Survey (archived at ICPSR, University of Michigan).

Reeves, R. (2022). *Of Boys and Men: Why the Modern Male Is Struggling, Why It Matters, and What to Do about It.* Washington, DC: Brookings.

Robnett, B., and Bany, J. A. (2011). Gender, Church Involvement, and African-American Political Participation. *Sociological Perspectives* 54(4), 689–712.

Rocha, R. R., Tolbert, C. J., Bowen, D. C., and Clark, C. J. (2010). Race and Turnout: Does Descriptive Representation in State Legislatures Increase Minority Voting? *Political Research Quarterly* 63(4), 890–907.

Rosenstone, S. J., and Hansen, J. M. (1993). *Mobilization, Participation, and Democracy in America.* New York: Macmillan.

Sanbonmatsu, K. (2006). *Where Women Run: Gender and Party in the States.* Ann Arbor: University of Michigan Press.

Sanbonmatsu, K. (2023). *The Donor Gap: Raising Women's Political Voices.* Center for American Women and Politics, Rutgers University, New Brunswick, NJ.

Sanchez, G. R. (2006). The Role of Group Consciousness in Political Participation among Latinos in the U.S. *American Politics Research* 34(4), 427–450.

Sanchez, G. R, and Foxworth, R. (2022). Social Justice and Native American Political Engagement. *Public Opinion Quarterly* 86(S1), 473–498.

Sanchez, G. R., Masuoka, N., and Abrams, B. (2019). Revisiting the Brown-Utility Heuristic: A Comparison of Latino Linked Fate in 2006 and 2016. *Politics, Groups, and Identities* 7(3), 673–683.

Sapiro, V. (1986). The Gender Basis of American Social Policy. *Political Science Quarterly* 101(2), 221–238.

Scarrow, S. E. (2007). Political Finance in Comparative Perspective. *Annual Review of Political Science* 10, 193–210.

Schlozman, K. L. (2002). Citizen Participation in America: What Do We Know? Why Do We Care? In *Political Science: The State of the Discipline*, Katznelson, I., and Milner, H. V., eds. New York: Norton, 433–461.

Schlozman, K. L., and Brady, H. E. (2022). Political Science and Political Participation. In *The Oxford Handbook of Political Participation*, Giugni, M., and Grasso, M., eds. New York: Oxford University Press, 26–44.

Schlozman, K. L., Brady, H. E., and Verba, S. (2018). *Unequal and Unrepresented: Political Inequality and the People's Voice in the New Gilded Age*. Princeton: Princeton University Press.

Schlozman, K. L., Burns, N., and Verba, S. (1994). Gender and the Pathways to Participation: The Role of Resources. *Journal of Politics* 56(4), 963–990.

Schlozman, K. L., Verba, S., and Brady, H. E. (2012). *The Unheavenly Chorus: Unequal Political Voice and the Broken Promise of American Democracy*. Princeton: Princeton University Press.

Schneider, M. C., Holman, M. R., Diekman, A. B., and McAndrew, T. (2016). Power, Conflict, and Community: How Gendered Views of Political Power Influence Women's Political Ambition. *Political Psychology* 37(4), 515–531.

Schur, L., Ameri, M., and Adya, M. (2017). Disability, Voter Turnout, and Polling Place Accessibility. *Social Science Quarterly* 98(5), 1374–1390.

Shames, S. L. (2015). American Women of Color and Rational Non-Candidacy: When Silent Citizenship Makes Politics Look Like Old White Men Shouting. *Citizenship Studies* 19(5), 553–569.

Shames, S. L. (2017). *Out of the Running: Why Millennials Reject Political Careers and Why it Matters*. New York: New York University Press.

Shaw, D., de la Garza, R. O., and Lee, J. (2000). Examining Latino Turnout in 1996: A Three-State, Validated Approach. *American Journal of Political Science* 44(2), 332–340.

Shear, M. D., and Sullivan, E. (2018). "Horseface, Lowlife, Fat, Ugly:" How the President Demeans Women. *New York Times*, October 16.

Shingles, R. D. (1981). Black Consciousness and Political Participation: The Missing Link. *American Political Science Review* 75(1), 76–91.

Simien, E. M. (2006). *Black Feminist Voices in Politics*. Albany: SUNY Press.

Simien, E. M. (2007). Doing Intersectionality Research: From Conceptual Issues to Practical Examples. *Politics & Gender* 3(2), 264–271.

Skocpol, T. (2017). Battle of the Mega-Donors: The Koch Network vs. Democracy Alliance. Retrieved from the University of Minnesota Digital Conservancy, hdl.handle.net/11299/194039.

Skocpol, T., and Fiorina, M. P., eds. (1999). *Civic Engagement in American Democracy*. Washington, DC: Brookings Institution.

Stockemer, D., and Sundstrom, A. (2023). The Gender Gap in Voter Turnout: An Artefact of Men's Over-Reporting in Survey Research? *The British Journal of Politics and International Relations* 25(1), 21–41.

Stokes, A. K. (2003). Latino Group Consciousness and Political Participation. *American Politics Research* 31(4), 361–378.

Tate, K. (1991.) Black Political Participation in the 1984 and 1988 Presidential Elections. *The American Political Science Review* 85(4), 1159–1176.

Tate, K. (1993). *From Protest to Politics*. Cambridge, MA: Harvard University Press.

Tate, K. (2004). *Black Faces in the Mirror*. Princeton: Princeton University Press.

Thomsen, D. M., and King, A. S. (2020). Women's Representation and the Gendered Pipeline to Power. *American Political Science Review* 114(4), 989–1000.

Thomsen, D. M., and Swers, M. L. (2017). Which Women Can Run? Gender, Partisanship, and Candidate Donor Networks. *Political Research Quarterly* 70(2), 449–463.

Tolley, E., Besco, R., and Sevi, S. (2022). Who Controls the Purse Strings? A Longitudinal Study of Gender and Donations in Canadian Politics. *Politics & Gender* 18(1), 244–272.

Traister, R. (2014). Why Are There No Female Sheldon Adelsons? *The New Republic*, July 23. newrepublic.com/article/118831/female-political-donors-why-there-no-lady-sheldon-adelson.

Traugott, M. W., and Katosh, J. P. (1979). Response Validity in Surveys of Voting Behavior. *Public Opinion Quarterly* 43(3), 359–377.

U.S. Bureau of Labor Statistics. (2021). Highlights of Women's Earnings in 2020. www.bls.gov/opub/reports/womens-earnings/2020/home.htm.

U.S. Bureau of Labor Statistics (2024). Usual Weekly Earnings Technical Note. www.bls.gov/news.release/wkyeng.tn.htm.

U.S. Census Bureau. (2020). Table H3. Households by Race and Hispanic Origin of Household Reference Person and Detailed Type. www2.census.gov/programs-surveys/demo/tables/families/2020/cps-2020/tabh3.xls.

U.S. Census Bureau. (2021). Data on 2020 Presidential Election Voting. www.census.gov/newsroom/press-releases/2021/2020-presidential-election-voting-and-registration-tables-now-available.html.

U.S. Census Bureau. (2024). State Population by Characteristics: 2020–2023. www.census.gov/data/tables/time-series/demo/popest/2020s-state-detail.html.

Uggen, C., Larson, R., Shannon, S., and Stewart, R. (2022). Locked out 2022: Estimates of People Denied Voting Rights. The Sentencing Project. www.sentencingproject.org/reports/locked-out-2022-estimates-of-people-denied-voting-rights/.

Uhlaner, C. J., and Scola, B. (2015). Collective Representation as a Mobilizer: Race/Ethnicity, Gender, and Their Intersections at the State Level. *State Politics and Policy Quarterly* 16(2), 227–263.

Verba, S., and Nie, N. H. (1972). *Participation in America*. New York: Harper and Row.

Verba, S., Burns, N., and Schlozman, K. L. (1997). Knowing and Caring about Politics: Gender and Political Engagement. *Journal of Politics* 59(4), 1051–1072.

Verba, S., Nie, N. H., and Kim, J.-O. (1978). *Participation and Political Equality: A Seven-Nation Comparison*. New York: Cambridge University Press.

Verba, S., Schlozman, K. L., and Brady, H. B. (1995). *Voice and Equality: Civic Voluntarism in American Politics*. Cambridge, MA: Harvard University Press.

Walsh, J. (2014). Politico Finds One More Reason for Women to Feel Guilty: No Koch Sisters! *Salon*, July 22. www.salon.com/2014/07/22/politico_finds_one_more_reason_for_women_to_feel_guilty_no_koch_sisters.

Washington, E. (2006). How Black Candidates Affect Voter Turnout. *Quarterly Journal of Economics* 121(3), 973–998.

Whitaker, L. D., ed. (2008). *Voting the Gender Gap*. Chicago: University of Illinois Press.

Whitby, K. J. (2007). The Effect of Black Descriptive Representation on Black Electoral Turnout in the 2004 Elections. *Social Science Quarterly* 88(4), 1010–1023.

White, I. K., and Laird, C. N. (2020). *Steadfast Democrats: How Social Forces Shape Black Political Behavior*. Princeton: Princeton University Press.

Williams, J. (2001). *Unbending Gender: Why Family and Work Conflict and What to Do about It*. New York: Oxford University Press.

Wolak, J. (2015). Candidate Gender and the Political Engagement of Women and Men. *American Politics Research* 43(5), 872–896.

Wolbrecht, C., and Campbell, D. E. (2017). Role Models Revisited: Youth, Novelty, and the Impact of Female Candidates. *Politics, Groups, and Identities* 5(3), 418–434.

Wolbrecht, C., and Corder, J. K. (2020). *A Century of Votes for Women*. New York: Cambridge University Press.

Wolfers, J., Quealy, K., and Leonhardt, D. (2015). The Methodology: 1.5 Million Missing Black Men. *The New York Times*. April 20.

Wolfinger, N. H., and Wolfinger, R. E. (2008). Family Structure and Voter Turnout. *Social Forces* 86(4), 513–1528.

Wolfinger, R. E., and Rosenstone, S. J. (1980). *Who Votes?* New Haven: Yale University Press.

Wong, J. S., Lien, P.-T., and Conway, M. M. (2005). Group-Based Resources and Political Participation among Asian Americans. *American Politics Research* 33(4), 545–576.

Wong, J. S., Ramakrishnan, S. K., Lee, T., and Junn, J. (2011). *Asian American Political Participation: Emerging Constituents and their Political Identities*. New York: Russell Sage Foundation.

Zukin, C., Keeter, S., Andolina, M., Jenkins, K, and Delli Carpini, M. (2006). *A New Engagement? Political Participation, Civic Life, and the Changing American Citizen*. New York: Oxford University Press.

Acknowledgments

To the memory of Scott and Sef Zeleznik

There is a story, probably apocryphal, about a renowned basso who received sustained, enthusiastic applause from the enraptured audience. After singing encore after encore, he bowed, turned to the audience, and apologized for being too exhausted to continue singing. A voice yelled out from the upper balcony, "You'll do it 'til you get it right."

This Element has its roots in a project that began a quarter of a century ago when Nancy and Kay – along with our co-author, Sidney Verba, and Shauna, then an undergraduate – published a book seeking to explain the persistent pattern such that men were somewhat more active in politics than women. Since then, joined, first, by Ashley, and more recently by Sara, we have returned periodically to this puzzle – not because we got it wrong then or in subsequent works, but because American politics and society have changed in ways having implications for gender inequalities in citizen participation. Along the way, we have incurred a lot of debts.

Our greatest debt is to Sidney, whom we lost about a year before the team rejoined forces to write this work. The guy who used to say facetiously, "I don't do research. I write books," taught us how to get from a good idea to publication: how to move from a substantive interest to a study design; how to use data to tell a story; how to recognize the magic moment when the endless pursuit of the perfect is producing diminishing returns. Perhaps more importantly, we learned from his example how to maintain high standards while behaving as decent and caring professionals and human beings. And the devoted and proud husband and father of three daughters was a feminist when his colleagues, who were not yet constrained by Title IX, were engaging unapologetically in multiple forms of discrimination against women.

One of the great pleasures of a project like this one is working with excellent students who help us as research assistants and, often, become part of the extended family. A quick glance at the acknowledgments to the first book from this project showed that, so many years later, we remain in touch with more than half the research assistants listed – who now include the Archivist of the United States, a public interest lawyer and seven tenured members of departments of political science. We are grateful to the students from several universities who assisted us so capably and cheerfully with the various data collections used in our analyses: from Boston College – Abigail Clifford,

Mackenzie Harrigan, John Henry Hobgood, Grace Jones, Mary Landers, John Loebs, Junwoo Kim, Jaehun Lee, Duncan MacKenzie, Jason Marcin, Madeleine McGrath, and Darya Treanor; from Boston University – Sabrina Abreu, Adeline Huang, Madison Phan, and Susannah Snellgrove; from Duke University – Haeji Cho Chatterjee, Megan Corey, Grace Davis, Megan Kaye, Jiewei Li, Mia Meier, Hannah Nelson, Claire Oh, Hannah Pechet, Michelle Schultze, Sadie Sheridan, Audrey Wang, Christina Wang, and Eldar Wang; from Harvard – Anna Menzel; from MIT– Jacqueline Park; and from Rutgers-Camden – Annalisa Klein and Brandon Vidales. We not only appreciate your efforts, but we are fortunate to have known you and hope that we have been able to reciprocate by helping you along the way.

Our thanks for institutional support to The University of Michigan's Political Science Department, whose generosity supported Sara's co-authorship and also allowed us to make this Element open access; and to Boston College and Boston University, both of which made it possible to support the students who worked with us.

Gary Jacobson generously shared his longitudinal data about congressional elections and candidates. We also took advantage of the data assembled by Bernard L. Fraga and Hans Hassell.

The adage about scholarly publication that "It is better to be criticized by your friends in manuscript than trashed by your enemies in print" once again proved apt. We are grateful for thoughtful feedback from Louise K. Davidson-Schmich and Amber N. Lusvardi, who served as Panel Chair and Discussant, respectively, as well as from other panelists and audience members, when we presented this project-in-progress at the 2021 Annual Meeting of the American Political Science Association. We appreciate the helpful readings and advice from Malliga Och and the astute comments from the anonymous readers for Cambridge University Press.

This publication would not have seen the light of day without the efforts and support of Tiffany Barnes and Diana O'Brien, editors for this exciting new Elements series on Gender & Politics, as well as Rachel Blaifeder, Jadyn Fauconier-Herry, Adam Hooper, and Sowmya Singaravelu at Cambridge University Press, and Krithika Shivakumar at Integra. This Element was in press before we knew the results of the 2024 elections.

Finally, this manuscript is a testament to women's resilience and capacity.

Work on this Element took place while life happened. Life that we were all carrying – not just the pandemic, but big things that life always involves – good and bad, things we chose, things life chose for us. Important, big things. Surgeries, moves, hospitalizations, birth, death, childcare, family care, family nurturing, family milestones, career milestones. Things we could not or would not want to put on pause. Our lives are all these things – our work ***and*** the people and lives we build and invest in – ***all*** of the interconnected parts of our lives. We are grateful to supportive spouses, partners, friends, and other essential helpers whose daily work enabled this research and writing – but ultimately, we know the solution must be institutional and not individual. May generations to come live in a nation with institutions and structures that enable and support such interconnected work for the long run.

Cambridge Elements ≡

Gender and Politics

Tiffany D. Barnes
University of Texas at Austin

Tiffany D. Barnes is Professor of Political Science at the University of Texas at Austin. She is the author of *Women, Politics, and Power: A Global Perspective* (Rowman & Littlefield, 2007) and, award-winning, *Gendering Legislative Behavior* (Cambridge University Press, 2016). Her research has been funded by the National Science Foundation (NSF) and recognized with numerous awards. Barnes is the former president of the Midwest Women's Caucus and founder and director of the Empirical Study of Gender (EGEN) network.

Diana Z. O'Brien
Washington University in St. Louis

Diana Z. O'Brien is the Bela Kornitzer Distinguished Professor of Political Science at Washington University in St. Louis. She specializes in the causes and consequences of women's political representation. Her award-winning research has been supported by the NSF and published in leading political science journals. O'Brien has also served as a Fulbright Visiting Professor, an associate editor at *Politics & Gender*, the president of the Midwest Women's Caucus, and a founding member of the EGEN network.

About the Series

From campaigns and elections to policymaking and political conflict, gender pervades every facet of politics. Elements in Gender and Politics features carefully theorized, empirically rigorous scholarship on gender and politics. The Elements both offer new perspectives on foundational questions in the field and identify and address emerging research areas.

Gender and Politics

Elements in the Series

In Love and at War: Marriage in Non-state Armed Groups
Hilary Matfess

Counter-Stereotypes and Attitudes toward Gender and LGBTQ Equality
Jae-Hee Jung and Margit Tavits

The Politics of Bathroom Access and Exclusion in the United States
Sara Chatfield

What's Happened to the Gender Gap in Political Activity? Social Structure, Politics, and Participation in the United States
Shauna L. Shames, Sara Morell, Ashley Jardina, Kay Lehman Schlozman and Nancy Burns

A full series listing is available at: www.cambridge.org/EGAP

For EU product safety concerns, contact us at Calle de José Abascal, 56-1°,
28003 Madrid, Spain or eugpsr@cambridge.org.

www.ingramcontent.com/pod-product-compliance
Lightning Source LLC
LaVergne TN
LVHW010302260326
834688LV00044B/1416